A Practical Guide to Advocacy in Family Proceedings

Second Edition

A Practical Guide to Advocacy in Family Proceedings

Second Edition

Stuart Barlow
LLB (London) Solicitor

Law Brief Publishing

Published 2024 by Law Brief Publishing, an imprint of Law Brief Publishing Ltd
30 The Parks
Minehead
Somerset
TA24 8BT

www.lawbriefpublishing.com

Paperback: 978-1-916698-53-6

This book is dedicated to my seven wonderful grandchildren: Bethany, Sam, Joseph, Rosie, Ava, Flynn and Halle for whom I am so thankful.

PREFACE

Advocacy in the Family Court is different from most other court arenas. No wigs, no gowns, no juries-and most hearings are behind closed doors. There are no rigid rules of evidence and cross examination is expected to be controlled and respectful. Usually there are no raised voices and finger pointing. Guilt and blame have their own special interpretation. It has a whole different flavour to the court room of the television and film screen and not what one would expect in a place where decisions are made which impact on the personal lives of thousands of people each day.

Family lawyers represent their clients in these court rooms where feelings are often running high and the outcome vital to their personal relationships. Yet, early training and preparation provided to the family advocate is rather thin on the ground. Universities and Law Schools focus mainly on the academic elements and give little time to the practicalities of how to present a case. When court advocacy is taught, the focus is often on criminal and civil courts perceived to be where most legal life is played out. Despite the number of family law cases listed before Judges and Lay Magistrates year by year, family court advocacy training is virtually non-existent; books and articles on the subject are few and far between.

For this reason, I have written a book that attempts to address this shortfall. It is intended for the real beginner. It assumes the reader to be new to family court advocacy but also provides information and guidance for those who practise in the Family Court regularly. It has less of the law, but more of the practice and procedure, often missing from a standard family law textbook.

I hope this book will help the beginner who is keen to do things right.

Advocates rarely learn on their own. They learn from others. I have had the immense privilege of working with and learning from court advocates over the years. One such solicitor was Neville Radcliffe, formerly of Browne Jacobson Solicitors, Nottingham, whose court advocacy I was able observe over some time. I am thankful for his inspiring example. I am also grateful to many others who have graciously corrected me when I have gone wrong and encouraged me on the occasions when I've needed help. There are too many to list here and some will not even realise how good they have been to me. Many thanks to all of them.

Special thanks to my wife Sue for her help in editing this book and correcting the mistakes in my grammar and style. Also to MBL Seminars who enabled me to rehearse part of the contents of this book when teaching lawyers from all over England and Wales in their seminars. Finally, I thank Law Brief Publishing who supported me in the writing of this book.

The law and procedure is correct as of 1st September 2024.

Stuart Barlow
September 2024

CONTENTS

INTRODUCTION

Solicitors prepare the case; barristers present it, was the maxim within the legal profession for many years. As recently as the 1970s few solicitors appeared in the courts as advocates. Those who did appear usually restricted themselves to minor criminal offences in the magistrates' court. Even though solicitors had a right of audience in other courts and tribunals, advocacy was undertaken by what was considered the elite performers at the Bar. Quite often, solicitors obtained their first practising certificates knowing little or nothing about the rules of evidence and how to appear in court. The solicitors' examinations did not cover this subject, presumably because it was a practical irrelevance. After all, barristers would be instructed to undertake any advocacy.

Has the situation changed over the years?

The Legal Practice Course, taught in many law schools to future solicitors, often covers skills in advocacy but only at a basic level and usually only in the fields of criminal and civil law. For those planning to practise family Law, a trainee's first encounter with any form of court advocacy is when he/she is sent off to court 'to sit behind Counsel.' They pick up the workings of the court by observation and follow up on that experience when they are sent on another court hearing a few weeks later.

Only after this does a trainee have the opportunity to consider whether court advocacy is for them. Some may be sent to court to represent a client on the basis that the attendance is 'only a Directions Hearing.'

By the time trainees qualify as a solicitor they often have little information or experience to make up their minds on the extent of their future career in family law. The newly qualified solicitor is frequently given a first real court encounter on the basis that they will 'either sink or swim.' Some law firms are conscientious in training their young family advocates but many are not. Prospective advocates frequently hold back in gaining further experience due to a lack of confidence, sometimes caused by a shortage of training and mentoring during their early years. Instructing Counsel is by far the easier option. Some solicitors even question the need to undertake their own advocacy at all.

This book is intended to give newly qualified solicitors and legal executives a helping hand in facing their first years in the court room. I hope the contents will give the practitioner details of the important parts of the law and procedure to equip them for advocacy from day one. The law and procedure is correct as of 1st September 2024.

CHAPTER ONE

WHY WE SHOULD UNDERTAKE OUR OWN ADVOCACY

1. Financial

Many firms expect their family lawyers to attend court as advocates because the financial rewards for the firm are greater. In legal aid cases, fees are proportionately higher for advocacy than the amount allowed for preparation. Usually, one fee is paid for attending a court hearing and this goes to the advocate. Keeping advocacy fees in-house, rather than paying a barrister, is often the preferred option. The same principle applies to privately paid work. Most clients cannot afford to pay for both solicitor and counsel. There may be other reasons to instruct a barrister but financial reward is high on the list.

2. Familiarity with the case and the client.

Advocates quite often deal with their family cases from the beginning. They see their client to give initial advice and follow this through to a court hearing. The solicitor becomes very familiar with the facts of the case and develops a close connection with the client. He/she should be the lawyer who is best placed to present the client's case to the court. Furthermore, the client has had consistent dealings with the solicitor and has gained their trust and confidence. To pass the hearing to another lawyer, especially at a late stage, can be a disappointment to the client.

3. Fulfilment

Once the advocate has acquired the necessary skills and experience in attending court as an advocate, the professional satisfaction can be enormous. To deal with a case and a client from beginning to end gives great satisfaction to the solicitor and also the client. This happens whatever the outcome of the court hearing.

4. Future Career

Solicitors move on to other firms to gain further expertise and prospects. Many prospective employers consider advocacy skills and experience a highly valued commodity and an important asset to their firm. They will often give substantial credit to those who are able and willing to undertake their own advocacy. Job adverts in the legal press reflect this position.

CHAPTER TWO

GETTING STARTED AS A FAMILY COURT ADVOCATE

It is undeniable that the more one appears in court as an advocate, the more capable one becomes. Practice makes perfect, at least in theory. However, the well-used approach of 'sink or swim' carries its dangers, not least for the client who is being used as an experiment in the art of advocacy.

Practice and preparation must be key to a lawyer becoming a better advocate. There are ways a potential advocate can prepare him/herself for the task ahead and at an early stage. But what sort of preparation?

Observation

This can begin as a trainee and also after qualification. The obvious example is when you attend court with counsel or an experienced member of your firm. Ask or even beg to be taken to court yourself to give you the opportunity to observe what happens before, during and after the hearing. Familiarise yourself with the case so you will know something about the facts.

Watching negotiations whilst at court can be an excellent way of learning how things are settled or otherwise. Take a note of what is said by the parties, advocates and the Judge who hears the case. The court hearing is likely to be in private so the chance to experience this will be limited. Ask questions of the advocates as to why things happen and the reasons for their actions. Ask why the Judge has said what he/she has said. Be interested and inquisitive. Observe the words and actions of the opposing parties. Think through the case and ask yourself whether you, even with your limited knowledge, would have arrived at the same conclusion.

Try to have a debrief after the hearing to clarify points you don't understand. You could explore the possibility of sitting with a District Judge for a day. That would be an ideal way of seeing how the court system works and have input from a real expert.

Advice

Shortly after qualifying as a solicitor I met with an experienced Lay Magistrate to seek his advice. I asked him 'What do you expect to see and hear when being addressed by an advocate in court?' He spent the next hour or so giving me his own personal views and observations as a Lay Magistrate. I went home and made a list of all the things he said. They were invaluable in my early years as an advocate and I still try to practise them today. I would recommend that you try this exercise. Many new to advocacy often have an abundance of colleagues around them who will readily share their own experiences. It is only a matter of asking them to help. Most will share their own stories with successes and failures and the odd horror story. You can learn so much from others for the price of a cup of coffee!

Know the Process

When you arrive at court it will be assumed that you are conversant with the relevant law and procedure. Any gaps in your knowledge should be filled in by you during your preparations. That is not to say you have to be encyclopaedic, but your understanding of the court process for your application is vital. Being familiar with the Family Procedure Rules, which apply in all family courts, is a starting point. The Red Book is an excellent authority which assists in most areas of Family Law and covers the law, procedure and case law.

Know your Case

Preparation is vital. This applies to all hearings; short or long; agreed or contested. Read the papers a couple of times and ask yourself the following:

- What order are you or your opponent requesting the court to make?
- Does the court have the power to make this order and what are the legal authorities?
- Do you or your opponent have the evidence in hand to support the case?
- Does your opponent's case fit with your own case and where do they clash?

Having gone through this exercise, talk the case through with an experienced colleague. Have you missed anything? Take on board the wise advice given to you.

Your first appearance in court may be stressful and you will walk out of the court building feeling relief that the ordeal is over, but there will also be a great sense of satisfaction and achievement. And it gets better as time goes on.

Following the hearing discuss the outcome with the same colleague as before. What could you have done to improve your performance and avoid the same mistakes?

And do the same next time.

Remember: An expert in anything was once a beginner.

CHAPTER THREE

TYPES OF TRIBUNAL

The Gatekeeper will decide on whether an application filed in the Family Court is suitable to be heard by the Lay Magistrates or by another court for example District Judge. In practice, many of the uncomplicated children cases are heard by Lay Magistrates, as are Non Molestation and Occupation Orders. An application can be transferred to another court at any stage in the proceedings. The Gatekeeper is likely to be a District Judge or a Court Legal Advisor who will read the court application and make a decision soon after it is filed.

Lay Magistrates with Legal Advisor

Usually three Lay Magistrates sit. They are not legally qualified but undertake some training to carry out their role. There will be a chairperson and two Magistrates 'on the wings'. The court hearing is in private and the court papers are confidential.

A court usher will be present in court who often wears a court black gown and carries a clip board with the list of cases attached to it. A Legal Advisor will be in court to assist the Lay Magistrates and advise on the law and procedure. He/she is likely to be a qualified lawyer and employed by HM Court Service.

Advocates address the chairperson not the Legal Advisor, even though the Legal Advisor is often involved in directing the proceedings.

Advocates will usually be seated on the front bench of the court room during the hearing unless the court directs otherwise. The parties will sit close to their lawyer usually immediately behind him/her or at their side. Only advocates are expected to address the court. The exception will be when a party is not legally represented. In this case, the unrepresented party, known as a Litigant in Person, will sit on the front bench and address the court personally.

Advocates will address the chairperson as "Sir" or "Madam". The Legal Advisor will call the case, briefly explain the nature of the application and then ask the advocate for the applicant to take matters forward. The applicant's advocate will introduce the parties and explain the reason for the hearing.

Types of Application

Most Private Children cases can be heard by Lay Magistrates. These include Section 8 applications: Child Arrangements Orders, Specific Issue Orders, Prohibitive Steps Orders. In addition, Special Guardianship and Adoption Orders are heard as well as applications for Non-Molestation and Occupation Orders. Certain financial orders can be heard by a Lay Magistrate but these are rare. Public Law Orders including Care and Supervision Orders, are frequently heard by Lay Magistrates.

The Hearing

The advocate for the applicant will present the case on behalf of his/her client by introducing the case, with reference to the Court Bundle.

Depending on the purpose of the hearing, the respondent will be asked to reply to the application by setting out the respondent's case.

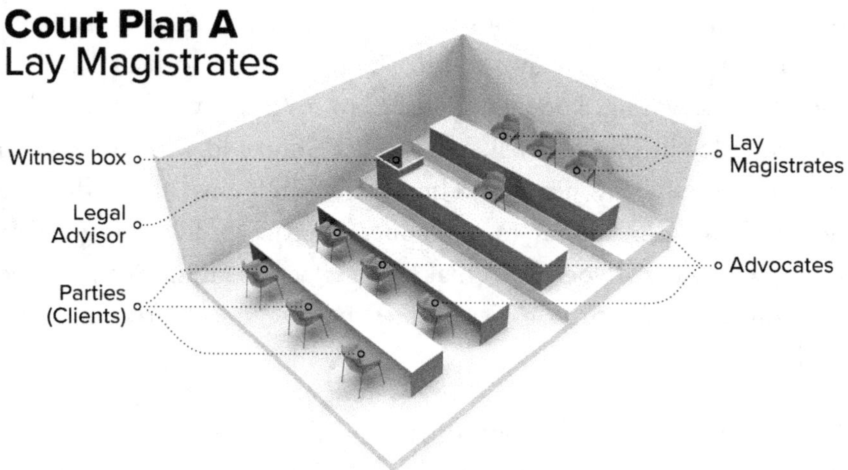

If the Lay Magistrates are being asked to decide on a particular issue immediately they will usually retire to their room to discuss matters and then return to court to announce their decision, giving reasons for making such an order. The court will often draft the court order and hand a copy the parties before they leave the court. If the court hears evidence on oath, a tape recording will be made of that evidence.

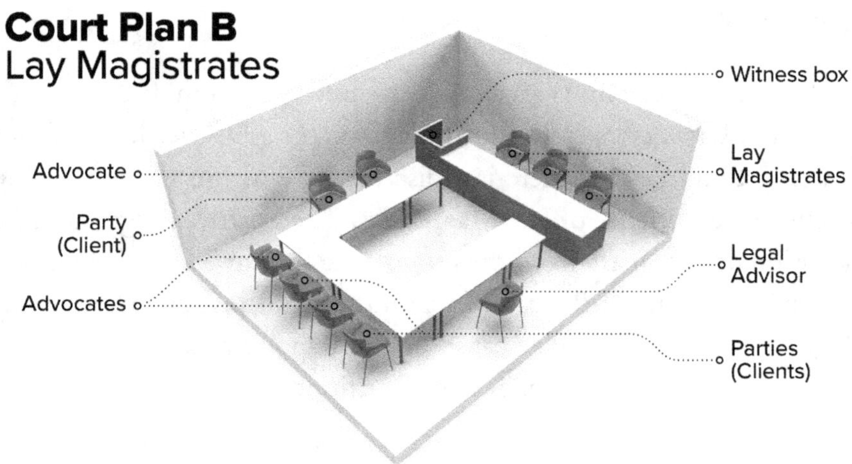

District Judge

A District Judge will hear cases that are often too complicated for the Lay Magistrates to deal with. The style of the hearing can be quite different to a hearing before Lay Magistrates. The District Judge is a qualified lawyer and is employed by the HM Court Service to hear family law cases. He/she will have practised family law for many years prior to being appointed to the court bench. He/she sits alone and will tend to take a proactive role in any hearing. The District Judge will be addressed as 'Judge'. This also applies to a Deputy District Judge. Some District Judges will allow advocates to make longer representations than others. They quite often express a view about the case at an early stage in the hearing.

If a decision is required about an issue in the proceedings, the District Judge will decide on this matter there and then and give reasons for doing so. The advocate will often be asked to draft the court order and submit this document to the court by email for approval by the District Judge. At some courts, hearings are conducted with all parties seated around a table with the District Judge at the head of the table. The arrangement of the court furniture can vary from court to court. The parties will sit alongside their advocate during the hearing. All hearings are tape recorded.

Types of Applications

A District Judge will hear cases that are often complex in law or procedure. Urgency may be a further reason for a District Judge to hear a case. It could be that there is a discreet issue within the proceedings beyond the experience of Lay Magistrates. The District Judge can make a decision on that matter and then transfer to the Lay Magistrates to hear the remaining part of the case. In addition to all matters heard by Lay Magistrates, a District Judge can hear court applications that flow from divorce proceedings including divorce petitions, financial and property applications as well as claims by cohabitants. Other applications relating to financial provision for children are within the remit of a District Judge.

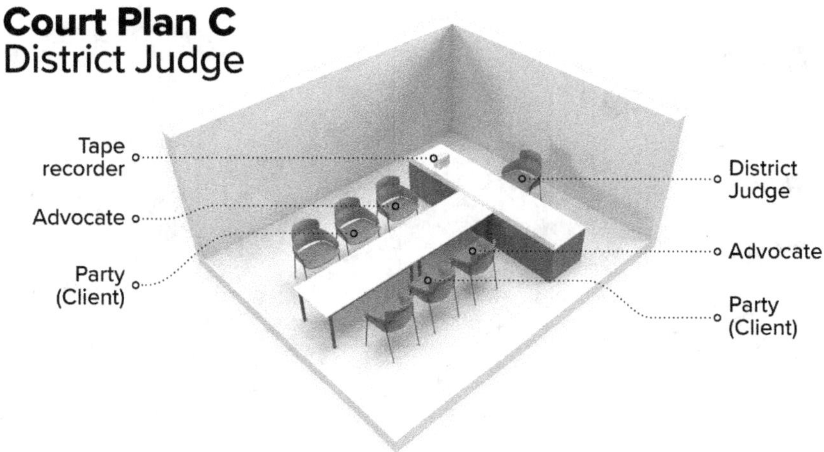

Circuit Judge

A Circuit Judge is the more senior Judge in a court circuit. Some have the title 'Designated Family Judge' who undertakes a supervisory role in overseeing the judicial work in a court area. The Circuit Judge is addressed as 'Your Honour.' This also applies to a Recorder who sits part time as a Circuit Judge.

An advocate sits on the front bench of the court room. He/she will stand to address the Judge but will remain seated during the other parts of the hearing. The parties will usually sit on the bench immediately behind their advocate.

Types of Application

A Circuit Judge is able to hear any case usually heard by Lay Magistrates or a District Judge, but is more likely to focus on more complex, long and more urgent family proceedings. Commonly, a Circuit Judge will handle complex Care Proceedings as well as appeals from a lower court.

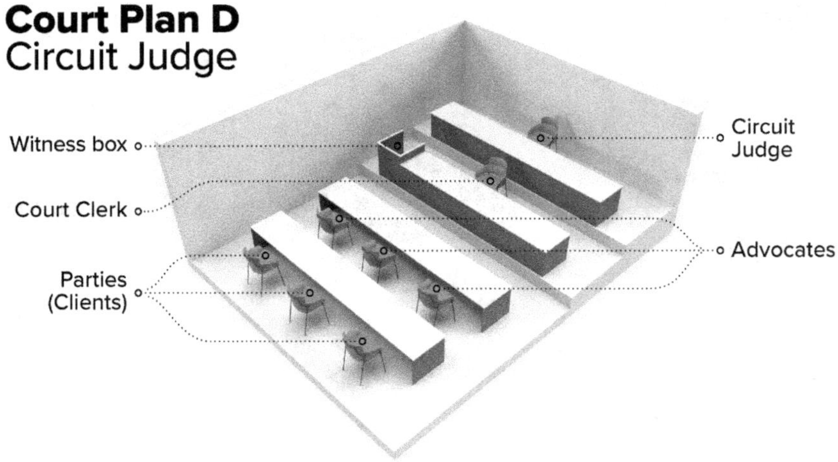

Judge or Lay Magistrates

Lay Magistrates are not qualified lawyers and whilst they undertake some training, their decisions are based on legal advice given to them by their Legal Advisor. They usually sit in cases that are more straight forward and make up a court bench of no less than two but usually three. Any decisions made will follow discussions in private and only after receiving legal advice from their Legal Advisor. As a result, hearings tend to take longer and their reasons are set out at length in writing. A District Judge will be a qualified lawyer with significant experience as a practising family lawyer. Thus, decision making is more immediate and succinct.

CHAPTER FOUR

HEARINGS AND THE FAMILY COURT ADVOCATE

Without Notice Hearings

In certain circumstances, an application can be made for the court to hear an application without the other party knowing about it. At a Without Notice Hearing the applicant must show that the making of the order is urgent. One example might be to prevent a party taking a child abroad before the hearing as it would not be safe if the applicant gave notice to the other party. A further example may be if an applicant has been threatened with abuse. During a Without Notice Hearing, the Judge will hear the applicant's reasons for making the application without informing the other party. The court may make the order requested or may postpone making the order until it has heard from the other party. Even if the court makes the order requested, it will usually set a date for a further hearing to decide whether or not the order should continue. The other party will be informed of this hearing date and asked to attend to put forward their views. The Without Notice Hearing is likely to take a more informal approach with the Judge reading the papers and making a decision often without hearing any formal evidence.

The advocate appearing for the applicant may have to make limited submissions but this will vary according to the case.

Directions Hearings

A Directions Hearing is listed for the Judge or Lay Magistrates to review the case and consider whether further information should be provided or action taken by the parties within the proceedings such as Cafcass or any other relevant body. Advocates representing the parties will usually meet together before the hearing to agree the terms of the court order and prepare a draft of the order. The court will consider the draft order and make any appropriate amendments. In the event of a disagreement between the parties, the Judge or Lay Magistrates will adjudicate on the matter. Representations by the advocates will often be in the form of submissions, frequently consenting to the terms of the agreed order. No evidence is heard. Judges and Lay Magistrates are encouraged to manage cases to ensure that the proceedings are progressed in the appropriate way.

The advocate should not assume that an agreement on the terms of a draft order will be 'rubber stamped' by the court and explanations are often required to justify the proposed order.

Case Management Hearings

Case management takes place when decisions are made by the court on such matters as:

- the key issues to be determined
- whether the proceedings should be listed for a fact finding hearing
- whether any interim orders need to made pending a final hearing
- whether directions are required to ensure the final hearing proceeds as planned.

The hearing takes a similar form to that of directions but is more structured and focussed in content. Case management is common in Care and Supervision Proceedings.

Contested Interim Hearings

Interim Orders can be made by the court until final orders are made. The hearing often takes the form of a full hearing when evidence is heard by the court and a decision is made pending the final decision of the court. Examples are: Interim Care or Interim Supervision Orders and Interim Child Arrangements Orders.

The advocate will be expected to prepare for a contested hearing, cross examine witnesses and make submissions to the court.

Fact Finding Hearings

If one party makes allegations during family law proceedings and the other party denies those allegations, the Judge will consider whether there should be a Fact Finding Hearing. This is a separate hearing arranged to decide whether or not the allegations are true. Fact Finding Hearings are most common in children cases, but can also take place during other family law proceedings such as for domestic abuse injunctions, divorce or financial remedies.

The advocate is expected to prepare for a contested hearing, cross examine witnesses and make submissions to the court.

Final Hearings

The final hearing brings the proceedings to an end. The Judge or Lay Magistrates will consider all of the available evidence. This includes evidence provided by the parties and any relevant reports provided by others such as Cafcass or the Local Authority. Using all of this information, the Judge will assess the evidence and come to a decision. The Judge may decide to make no order or make an order requested by the parties. The format of the final hearing can take various forms: an Agreed Order, a Contested Hearing (when evidence is heard) or a hearing where the parties make oral submissions without any evidence being called. This depends on the nature of the final hearing.

The advocate is expected to prepare for a contested hearing, cross examine witnesses and make submissions to court as to what orders should be made.

CHAPTER FIVE

PRE-PROCEEDINGS

Negotiation

"It is incumbent upon both parties to negotiate, if possible, and at least make attempts to settle ..." Gojkovic v Gojkovic (No 2) (1991) 2 FLR 233

It is usually in the interest of all the parties to attempt to settle disputes in family matters. Courts encourage disputing parties to attempt to resolve matters without the need for a contested hearing. This frequently gives rise to more satisfied clients, more satisfactory outcomes and the removal of uncertainty of outcome. Issuing proceedings in the Family Court should be considered as a last resort after parties have exhausted other means of ending a dispute. The courts expect that parties involved in a dispute to make every effort to resolve their dispute before they make a decision to issue proceedings. This might involve:

- Speaking to the other party in an attempt to settle some, or all, of the issues.

- If initial direct conversations fail, a party should be prepared to put their side of the dispute in writing and allow time for the other party to respond.

- Explore Mediation, which is a process by which opposing parties are brought together with the aim of finding a workable agreement to avoid recourse to the courts.

Alternatives to court proceedings

Mediation

Mediation is a form of negotiation facilitated by a neutral third party within a structured process. The parties agree to the appointment of an impartial third person to assist them to communicate better with one another and reach their own agreed and informed decisions concerning some, or all, of the issues relating to separation, divorce, children, finance or property by negotiation.

- Mediators are independent and impartial, qualified professionals with a range of backgrounds from law to healthcare. They work to facilitate a settlement which is tailored to the parties' needs and interests rather than imposing or deciding the final outcome. Mediators can assist with communication and help reduce conflict and dispute going forward. Their role is to organise the process, facilitate the process and act as an intermediary between the parties.

- Mediation can take place at any stage of the dispute but it is most effective at an early stage. The President of the Family Division is keen to promote mediation and it is an important plank of the 'Supporting Separating Family Alliance' proposed by the second report of the Working Group on Private Law Cases chaired by Cobb J (12 March 2020).

    (i) A mediation agreement should be entered into at the start. The agreement will include practical matters, mediator's fees, confidentiality clause, immunity clause etc. Typically mediation goes through four stages: opening: open meeting where there is an introduction, parties' opening positions and mediator's remarks;

(ii) exploration: through a combination of open and closed meetings where the mediator explores the issues and strategies for settlement;

(iii) negotiation: mostly through closed meetings the mediator acts as a broker between parties who consider and make offers, and helps parties work through deadlock;

(iv) closing: open meeting to confirm terms of settlement or summarise the closing positions if settlement is not reached.

(v) If an agreement is reached, the mediator will draw up a Memorandum of Understanding. This can then be made legally binding by the court in the form of a consent order.

www.lawsociety.org.uk/support-services/advice/articles/consent-order-guidance/

- **Mediation Vouchers**

On 26 March 2021, the Ministry of Justice launched a mediation voucher scheme which will contribute up to £500 towards mediation costs in eligible cases. On attendance at a MIAM, the mediator will assess whether a party meets the eligibility requirements. The case types for which a voucher may be claimed are a dispute/application relating to a child or a dispute/application regarding family financial matters which also involves a dispute/application relating to a child.

Practice Direction 36V – Pilot Scheme: Family Mediation Voucher Scheme, published on 26 March 2021.

www.familymediationcouncil.org.uk/mediation-voucher-scheme

- **Mediation must be attempted in earnest**

A Judge may to refuse to hear a case where mediation has not been attempted. The Judge may adjourn a case, at any stage, for mediation to be attempted. Parties are expected, now more than ever, to try mediation earnestly (***Re B (a child) (Unnecessary Private Law Applications) [2020]***). The Judge warned parties and lawyers against making unnecessary applications. Part of a solicitor's role is to persuade clients that going to court really is a last resort.

- **Mediation Information and Assessment Meetings (MIAMs)**

s10(1) Children and Families Act 2014 provides that: *Before making a relevant family application, a person must attend a family mediation information and assessment meeting.* This means that MIAMs are compulsory and so all clients will be expected to attend such a meeting before making an application to the court. A *relevant family application* is defined by **s10(3)** as an application which (a) is made to the court in, or to initiate, family proceedings and (b) is of a description specified in **FPR**. This will include all the most usual applications in private law proceedings relating to children and in proceedings for a financial remedy.

(a) A MIAM is a meeting with a specially qualified family mediator, who can explain the alternatives to the court process. Divorcing and separating couples who want to use the court process to resolve any questions about children or money have to show that they have attended a MIAM before they can apply for a court order. Most applications to the Single Family Court require the **Form FM1** confirming mediation has been attempted before they will issue proceedings or a Judge may adjourn a case for the parties to attempt mediation before he will allow the case to proceed.

(b) At a MIAM a qualified family mediator will discuss the client's situation on a confidential basis. If a client is unsure of the process, they may wish to book an individual mediation session to examine how they feel about the process. Usually this is a one-to-one meeting, although sometimes parties attend together if they wish. Currently, only one of the parties is required to attend a MIAM to talk through the alternatives to court and decide whether another route could be appropriate.

(c) If the client has a low income and relatively low capital, they may be entitled to legal aid although not all mediators will conduct legal aid matters.

(https://thefma.co.uk/)(https://www.familymediationcouncil.org.uk).

- **Exemptions to mediation**

A party will not be expected to attend a MIAM if any of the following apply to the situation:

- A party has made an allegation of domestic violence against the other supported by clear evidence.
- An application to the court needs to be made urgently because there is a risk to the life or safety of the person who is making the application.
- The dispute is about money and either party is bankrupt.
- Social Services are involved because there are concerns about the safety and wellbeing of a child.
- In the past four months mediation has been unsuccessfully attempted.
- A mediator signs **Form FM1** confirming that mediation is not suitable, this form must be sent to the court when issuing most family law applications

(https://www.gov.uk/government/publications/give-information-for-a-family-mediation-assessment-form-fm1).

Recent Changes

The Family Procedure Rules (FPR) have been updated and, amongst other things, make several changes to improve the level of attendance at mediator initial assessment meetings (MIAMs) by applicants to certain family proceedings. The changes have been introduced because the previous rules were not applied to the extent expected and did not divert cases from court proceedings to the degree that had been intended.

Under the previous rules, it was a requirement for all prospective applicants to attend a MIAM, unless an exemption applies. The rule changes arise from a push to help more parties settle their cases outside of court.

The Family Procedure (Amendment No. 2) Rules 2023, which come into force in April 2024, amend the Family Procedure Rules 2010 Rules 2 and 4 came into force on 8 April 2024, and rule 3 and rules 5 to 19 came into force on 29 April 2024.

Key changes in the FPR rules

Informative requirement

The definition included in the rules not only widens the scope for non-court dispute resolution, but also amends FPR 3.9(2), which mandates MIAMS providers to inform their clients about suitable forms of non-court dispute resolution and provide comprehensive materials on each option. This requirement ensures that parties are well-informed about all the available alternatives to court proceedings.

Broader definition of domestic abuse

The definition of "domestic violence" within the FPR has been broadened to "domestic abuse," aligning with the provisions of the Domestic Abuse Act 2021. Furthermore, FPR 3.8(1)(c)(ii) now considers "significant financial hardship" instead of "unreasonable hardship" in cases involving domestic abuse. There will still be an exemption where there has been domestic abuse and allow parties to advance straight to court proceedings.

Ongoing consideration of non-court resolution

Perhaps the most significant change is that parties are now obligated to consider non-court dispute resolution not only before initiating a case but also throughout its duration. FPR 3.3(1A) requires parties to file a form with the court and serve it on all parties, expressing their views on non-court dispute resolution. This ensures continuous evaluation of alternative methods to resolve issues and reinforces the duty on Judges to continue to question if alternative methods should be tried throughout the case. This also sets up the court to understand the parties 'views and question why a party may be opposed to alternative methods without good reason.

Without a doubt the changes are being implemented so that court users, Judges and lawyers have mediation and other non-court dispute resolution approaches at the forefront of their minds when considering the court, as a means to resolve disputes. While the practical implementation of these changes remains to be seen, initiatives such as the Pathfinder Pilot in North Wales and judicial endorsements of non-court dispute resolution, as seen in the case of **X vs Y [2024] EWHC 538 (FAM)**, where Mrs Justice Knowles endorsed the use of non-court dispute resolution, referring specifically to the new rules, provide promising indications for the future.

Removal of agreement requirement

Previously, cases could be adjourned if parties agreed to consider non-court dispute resolution. However, this requirement (FPR3.4(1)(b) was deleted from the 29 April and amended rule, FPR 3.4 (1A) will exist. This rule allows the court to adjourn proceedings to facilitate non-court resolution where "timetabling of proceedings allows sufficient time for these steps to be taken" without explicit agreement from the parties. What is not clear is if the parties can be forced to attend. However, if the parties fail to attend, FRP 28.3(7) is now amended to state that failure to engage without good reason may lead to a departure from "no order as to costs". What is also not clear is what is a "good reason" and at what stage could a court pause or delay proceedings to consider alternative methods. This provision incentivises active participation in alternative methods and discourages unjustified resistance.

Costs

The general rule as to how costs are treated in financial remedy proceedings is that, usually, each party is to bear their own costs, although it is in the court's power to order one party to pay the other party's costs where it considers it appropriate to do so as a result of their conduct. The scope of such conduct is to be expanded to include failure, without good reason, to attend non-court dispute resolution. Parties embarking on court proceedings will need to be alive to this costs risk if they have not reasonably engaged in other dispute resolution methods. Whilst the new rules undoubtedly strengthen the court's focus on non-court dispute resolution in line with the general trend towards the same, they do not go as far as mandating the use of such means.

See Chapter Five for more details on the FPR and changes.

Collaborative law

- Collaborative law is a process in which lawyers and clients work together to resolve a dispute. It aims to address all legal, financial and practical aspects of separation and the parties' future relationship.

- It is most suitable where parties are focused on their children's best interests and/or maintaining or developing a good relationship, and are seeking a solution outside the court process. There must be a constructive and respectful approach with both parties willing to give full disclosure.

- When the collaborative process ends the lawyers can no longer act for the parties.

The process can be broken down into four stages:

1. preparation meetings, include: — between each solicitor and client for the solicitor to explain the process, and discuss goals and objectives, and — between the solicitor separately to plan the first meeting;

2. initial four-way meeting is between all solicitors and clients where the parties seek to Lay the foundations and share their objectives. An agenda will be set for the next meeting. Solicitors and clients will sign a four-way agreement committing to work out a settlement without going to court;

3. intermediate four-way meetings may be held before all issues are resolved. Each meeting will have an agenda, review progress and revise key issues. Part of their function is for information sharing and gathering. There may be involvement of other professionals such as accountants, pension experts, independent social workers. The lawyers will assist the clients in exploring their options and devising solutions;

4. final four-way meeting happens when an agreement is reached. It will deal with formalities of signing documents. Clients can withdraw from the process at any time but there is usually a cooling off period before proceedings can be initiated. The negotiations cannot be then referred to in evidence.

www.resolution.org.uk/collaborative_process/

Arbitration

- Arbitration offers the opportunity for parties to agree to appoint an independent, qualified professional to adjudicate their dispute and make a binding decision.

- The same arbitrator can deal with all stages of the case from start to finish. This continuity provides reassurance for the parties that the person making the decisions in their case has a real understanding of their situation. Additionally, the parties can have much greater input into how the proceedings are run. This can include whether to meet face to face or in writing only. One benefit is that the parties can use the arbitrator for the whole process. This can also save great expense.

- Arbitration is often quicker and cheaper than the court process. It offers flexibility and privacy. The unique factor is that arbitration offers finality, although in **Haley v Haley [2020] EWCA Civ 1369** the Court of Appeal clarified the route whereby an aggrieved party may challenge an arbitral award and the judgment confirms that the court retains a supervisory jurisdiction under the Matrimonial Causes Act 1973.

The court suggested the primary means for challenging an arbitral award should be under the Arbitration Act 1996.

ifla.org.uk/cms/wp-content/uploads/2015/09/Public.pdf

www.familylawweek.co.uk/site.aspx?i=ed126784

Funding & Costs

Legal Aid is available to some individuals who need to take legal advice and representation but who cannot otherwise afford it. Legal Aid has been severely restricted in recent years, and individuals today need to satisfy certain requirements such as their income level, before they are awarded Legal Aid. Public funding will only be given if there is a strong benefit to the client and the applicant has suffered domestic abuse. In public law applications Legal Aid is available to parents and others who have parental responsibility in respect of a child who is involved in the court proceedings on a non-means and non-merits basis.

The other option is for the client to receive legal advice on a private fee-paying basis. Some family lawyers may charge fees at an hourly rate, while others may provide services on a fixed fee basis.

It is unusual for the court to award costs against the unsuccessful party in family proceedings but if the court is satisfied that a party has conducted himself/herself in an unacceptable way, it can order him/her to pay part or all of their opponent's costs.

See Chapters Thirty and Thirty-One for more details on funding and costs

CHAPTER SIX

WHEN YOU ARRIVE AT COURT

Security Check

For those attending a court hearing, bags and pockets will be checked as they would be at an airport. This may include: emptying pockets into a tray, taking off shoes, coat, gloves, hat or belt and walking through an archway detector or being checked with a handheld scanner. Security staff will keep any items not taken into the building and lawyers will be given a receipt. In some courts advocates in possession of a permit may be entitled to fast track the queue.

Court Lists

In most courts there is a list of cases on the wall near the entrance or reception desk. This list usually shows where the case is to be heard, giving the court number, the time of the hearing and the name of the Judge who will deal with the case. The purpose of the list is to enable parties and their advocates to identify easily when and where the case is to be heard. In family cases, the names of the parties are not always listed but the case is identified by the case number set out in the court documents.

Usher

Court Ushers are court employees who make sure that everyone involved with a court case is present and that they know what to do. Their day-to-day responsibilities include: ensuring that the courtroom is prepared for the hearing, greeting those coming to court for hearings, calling witnesses and parties into court and directing witnesses in the taking of oaths. An usher is often identified by the wearing of a court gown and carrying a clip board with a court list attached.

Waiting areas

Public waiting areas are usually accessible from the main public entrances. Seating areas are also provided. Public toilets, pay telephones, and water fountains are often located near these areas. Waiting space varies according to court in question. A public address system facilitates moving people from the waiting area to the court rooms at the appropriate times. In some courts large numbers of people can be found waiting for their case to be called with no place to sit. This can sometimes be a problem creating a lack of privacy.

Interview rooms

Whilst most courts have private interview rooms for advocates to meet with their clients, there is often a limited number available, and advocates may need to see their clients elsewhere in the court building.

Court Clerk

The Court Clerk is a court employee and sits in front of the Judge's bench. He/she helps the Judge make sure the case runs smoothly. They keep a record of the hearing including a note of people attending.

Legal Advisor

A Legal Advisor is a legally qualified person who helps Lay Magistrates apply the law and procedure in the Family Court. They do not play any part in the decision making process, but are there to advise the court on points of law and procedure. In addition, Legal Advisors are able to carry out the 'Gate Keeper' function to determine which court will hear a case. The Legal Advisor can make certain procedural orders which are uncontroversial or agreed, as well as sit to hear first hearings in Private Children cases.

CHAPTER SEVEN

PREPARATION FOR THE COURT HEARING

Four pointers as you go to Court:

1. Preparation is essential for every hearing, even for short and interim hearings.

2. Be clear about what orders you are asking the court to make.

The application to the court will dictate this but consideration should be given to other options just in case the original application is unsuccessful. For example, the court may refuse an order for unsupervised direct contact but may be willing to consider supervised contact. The court has a wide discretion to consider other options, so your preparation should take this into account.

The court must have the power to make the order you are seeking. Familiarise yourself with the most common statutes and court rules.

When making a Financial Order, the court has a duty to consider whether it has:

- Power e.g. ss 22 – 24 MCA; and

- Jurisdiction e.g. after decree nisi for final orders; and

- It is fair and reasonable e.g. within the section 25 criteria.

Note that the court has no additional powers simply because there is an agreement between the parties.

The most common statutes and court rules are:

Family Procedure Rules 2010 with amendments are a single set of rules which govern the procedures used in family courts in England and Wales

The Matrimonial Causes Act 1973 is the main legislation relating to divorce and financial proceedings.

The Civil Partnership Act 2004 which allows same-sex couples to form registered civil partnerships

The Child Support Act 1991 covers statutory child maintenance

Schedule 1 to the Children Act 1989 allows the court to make financial and property orders for the benefit of a child.

The Inheritance (Provision for Family and Dependants) Act 1975 which allows a court to vary and extend the distribution of the estate of a deceased person's will or the standard rules of intestacy to make financial provision for a spouse, civil partner or cohabitee.

The Matrimonial and Family Proceedings Act 1984 and Schedule 7 to the Civil Partnership Act 2004

The Trusts of Land and Appointment of Trustees Act 1996 (TOLATA) allows the court to determine the extent of each party's interest in land or property, how that property can be dealt with and order sale of the property.

The Married Women's **Property Act 1882 and ss 67, 68 and 74 of the Civil Partnership Act 2004** covers property rights of the married women and civil partners.

In Children cases the most common authorities:

Family Procedure Rules 2010 with amendments are a single set of rules which govern the procedures used in family courts in England and Wales

Children Act 1989 (as amended) is the primary source of law in relation to children, their upbringing and welfare.

Adoption and Children Act 2002 amongst other things include Special Guardianship Orders and which allows unmarried people and same sex couples to adopt children.

Practice Direction 12B The Child Arrangements Programme (CAP) made up of 23 paragraphs that give a full picture of how that court process works.

Practice Direction 12J Child Arrangements & Contact Orders:

Domestic Abuse and Harm (PD12J) sets out what the court is required to do in cases where there is an allegation of domestic abuse.

In Injunction cases the authorities are:

Family Law Act 1996 Part IV in relation to family homes and domestic abuse

Family Procedure Rules 2010 with amendments are a single set of rules which govern the procedures used in family courts in England and Wales

3. You have Evidence in support of your client's case.

Your Court Bundle should contain papers that support the making of the order you seek. If further evidence is required, you will need to consider what directions are required to bring this before the court.

4. Ensure the Court Bundle is prepared, filed and saved in the correct form and in accordance with the court rules.

CHAPTER EIGHT

TEN BASIC TIPS WHEN ATTENDING COURT

- Dress correctly.
- Prepare fully for the hearing.
- Arrive at court early so you can speak to your client and your opponent to negotiate.
- Find a meeting room for discussions
- Introduce yourself to your opponent, write his/her name on your note pad. You will need the details when presenting your case in court.
- Keep your client informed throughout the course of hearing.
- Ensure you address the bench correctly.
- Make sure your Court Bundle is in the correct form and sufficient copies have been provided for the court and the witness box.
- During the hearing, speak slowly and politely to the court and to your opponent.
- In court, never become argumentative, show exasperation or become angry.

CHAPTER NINE

FAMILY COURT HEARINGS

Bowing in court

As persons enter the court room, whether court officials, lawyers or members of the public, it is customary to bow to the Royal Coat of Arms and indirectly those presiding over the case. This is in recognition of the fact that justice stems from the Monarch and that Law Courts are part of the Royal Court. Those present in court should stand up from their seat when the Judge or Lay Magistrates enters the room. "All Rise" will be declared, to show respect for them as representatives of the Crown.

Those who can come into the court room

The general rule is that family cases are heard in private. The exceptions are: Divorce hearings; Contempt of Court applications; Committal Order applications.

In certain types of cases, the court has the power to direct that the case be heard in open court, for example, Non-Molestation applications.

The general public are not allowed in court. Family members or friends are not usually permitted into the court room. Children are usually left outside the court room.

The only people normally allowed in court are :

- The parties in the court proceedings being heard
- The lawyers for the parties

- The Judge and the court staff
- Cafcass officers or Local Authority social workers
- Witnesses, whilst they are giving evidence
- The media, although the court can exclude their attendance in certain cases
- An Interpreter
- A McKenzie Friend with the permission of the court
- Anyone else with the permission of the court eg a supporter for one of the parties who is vulnerable.

Those who can see the court papers

Children cases: the court papers should be treated as confidential. Rules 12.73 to 12.75 FPR and Practice Direction 12G.

The papers can be shown to a legal advisor or any other person assisting in the preparation of a party's case, for example a McKenzie Friend, who should be bound by the confidentiality rule. Court judgements are also private unless the court gives permission to share them with another person. Court orders can be shown to other people unless the court directs otherwise.

Money cases: the financial information contained in the papers should only be used for the purposes of the proceedings and should be treated as private. They should not be shown to anyone else without the permission of the court. The court can give permission for the papers in family proceedings to be shown to a person outside the court proceedings but will set out details in a court order.

Recordings of the Court Hearing

All court proceedings are audio recorded. The making of a recording is now a part of the Family Procedure Rules rule 27.9 which requires a recording to be made of a hearing. Most Courts now record digitally with court staff logging and downloading the day's audio recordings onto DVD at the end of the court day. This recording will be made of the whole hearing, including any part where the Judge gives a judgment.

Other than pressing stop and start, Judges have no involvement with the process of recording and storage of the official recordings. When a transcript request is made this is dealt with by court staff. It will be court staff who will locate the disc and convey it to the transcription company.

The parties to a case do not have the general right to listen to or obtain a copy of the actual recording of a hearing and they are prohibited from making their own unless the Judge gives permission Section 9 Contempt of Court Act 1981. A party can ask for permission to obtain a transcript of the recording on payment of a fee.

Interpreters

The Family Court will, if necessary, provide an interpreter if the case involves children, domestic violence or forced marriage. A party might still be able to have an interpreter if he/she can't afford to pay for an interpreter, don't qualify for legal aid and don't have a friend or family member whom the Judge permits to act as your interpreter. If a party is deaf or hard of hearing, an interpreter will be made available.

Video Link Evidence

A video link in court allows a witness to give evidence from a remote location via video. They will appear on-screen in the courtroom and a camera in the court will allow them to also monitor the proceedings. Arrangements will be made by the court staff following a direction of the court.

Electronic devices

Before entering court all electronic devices must be turned off. It is a criminal offence to use mobile phones or undertake any recording of proceedings.

CHAPTER TEN

THE COURT HEARING ITSELF

A typical hearing will have the following format:

1. Introductions given by the applicant's advocate who will introduce the parties and advocates by name:

   Morning Sir/Madam. My name is Simon Smith and I represent the applicant in these proceedings. My client sits behind me. The respondent is represented by Mrs June Baker and her client is sitting behind her.

2. Opening by the applicant's advocate who gives a brief introduction to the case and the reason for the court hearing. If there are case summaries prepared and the Judge has read the papers, the opening can be very brief. At this point, the Judge (or Lay Magistrates) or any other lawyer will often check that the court has the full set of papers including papers filed at a late stage:

   > 'Could I please check Sir/Madam that you have received all the papers in this case and that you have had an opportunity of reading them'.

3. If the papers are agreed, what happens next in the case will depend on the purpose of the hearing before the court. If the court is being asked to make a directions order, the applicant will usually present a set of agreed directions to be considered by the court.

   If the hearing is a Financial Dispute Resolution Hearing, the hearing will comprise of both parties' advocates making oral submissions, after which the District Judge will give his/her views as to how the case should be settled.

If the court is being asked to make a decision on the evidence before it, the hearing will proceed in a particular way.

4. Evidence hearings In a Private Children case: if there is any evidence from a social worker, Cafcass officer or expert witness, the court will need to make an early decision as when to hear their evidence. More commonly, their evidence is heard first.

   Once the professional or expert witnesses have been dealt with, the applicant will usually give evidence, followed by any witnesses called by the applicant.

   Each witness will give their evidence-in-chief on oath, based on their previously made written statement and will be subject to cross examination by the other parties. The Judge may also ask some questions of the witness. Some judges will say very little whilst the case is being presented but others will be proactive by asking regular questions of both the witnesses and the lawyers.

   The respondent will usually give evidence next, followed by the respondent's witnesses.

   The order of witness evidence might change if the evidence relates mainly to allegations made by one party against the other. A Finding of Fact Hearing is an example. If this is the case, the person making the allegations should usually give evidence first, so the person about whom the allegations are made has the chance to hear the accusations before responding.

5. The Judge/Lay Magistrates will hear Closing speeches (submissions) from the advocates of each party, the respondent first and applicant second. In a Care case, the advocate for the children will address the court last.

6. The Judge/Lay Magistrates will give a Judgment. This may be immediate (extempore) or after a short break or may be 'handed down' on a later date in court or by email if this is agreed by the parties.

7. Once Judgment has been given the Judge/Lay Magistrates will hear any argument about costs (usually rare) or any application for permission to appeal.

Summary

- Introductions and Opening by the applicant's advocate.
- Applicant gives evidence on oath.
- Cross-examination of applicant by respondent's advocate.
- Witnesses for applicant gives evidence on oath and cross-examined.
- End of applicant's case.
- Repeat exercise for respondent.
- Submissions and speeches by parties.
- Decision of court.
- Applications for costs and permission to appeal.

Submissions

In the Family Court, the act of presenting arguments is known as making Submissions. They are usually made orally. A Submission is your speech to the court, putting forward your client's case. A Submission is simply a coherent argument intended to persuade the court to find in your clients' favour.

In most family cases, the applicant will make his/her Opening Submissions at the beginning of the case and at the end of the evidence make Closing Submissions. Advocates for the other parties will also make Closing Submissions.

Submissions at the end of the case is when you present your arguments about the effects of the evidence which has been presented to the court and why it should find in your favour. At that stage you might, for example, set out the reasons why you say that the court should prefer the evidence of your witnesses to the evidence for the other side. It is also the stage when you tell the court what you say is the correct legal approach to the facts in your case.

Submissions may, however, be made at other stages of a case. Where there is a debate about a question of law, the arguments are also referred to as Submissions.

In some cases, the court may ask for a Written Outline of Submissions to be sent in before a hearing. This is intended to save time at the hearing. Advance warning allows both the court and your opponent to consider the arguments fully and helps ensure that the parties fully understand all the points made at the hearing of the oral submissions.

At a Submissions-Only Hearing the Judge or Lay Magistrates will decide on the matters in dispute based on the evidence and statements filed before the hearing. The Judge or Lay Magistrates might also ask you and the other parties questions. Matters must be decided on the basis only of Submissions (Written or Oral) by the parties, so no witnesses are be called and no cross-examination of the parties takes place.

Cross-examination of Witnesses

The Family Court will use the Court Bundle when hearing the case. Usually, the only evidence it hears will be contained in that Bundle. In theory, there should be no surprises and the points in issue should be clear to see from the papers. Additional points of evidence can only be introduced in Examination in Chief with the permission of the court. This is reassuring as you should not normally be faced with new information or fresh evidence of which you have no prior notice. The exception to this rule is evidence that updates the court as to information already contained in the Court Bundle. This enables you to prepare your cross-examination questions and establish a planned structure to your questioning in advance of the hearing.

The Purpose of Cross-Examination is:

- To elicit evidence in support of your case
- Cast doubt on or undermine the witness's evidence
- To challenge disputed evidence.

When preparing your case, list the key issues the court is being asked to determine. Identifying these will help you prepare questions for cross-examination.

Your cross-examination should:

- Be well structured – examine the witness evidence and make a list of the things that you want to achieve in your cross-examination
- Contain short and clear questions so that the witness and the court understand them
- End when you've made your point – avoid asking too many questions that would allow the witness to regain lost ground. Do

not feel you have to ask every possible question. Focus on the relevant issues.

You do not have to cross examine, but you must make it clear that you do not necessarily accept the evidence put forward. If this is made clear in your client's evidence to the court, detailed cross examination may not be required. If on the other hand, your client does not deal fully with the issue in his/her statement or matters are in dispute, cross examination is important. Remember that by asking a question in cross examination, there is a danger this can do more harm than good. The witness may be able to re-enforce his/her evidence and come over in a more convincing way.

Cross-examination is a skill that must be developed with experience, but the following apply in most cases:

- Never ask a question to which you don't know the answer. Cross examination is no place to experiment. The answer could damage your case

- Always ask leading questions to which the answer is yes or no. Open ended questions will give the witness the opportunity to say whatever they like and at length. You lose control of the questioning and could harm your case in the process

- Ask questions in small pieces so you can obtain an answer to each part. You can then measure the need to follow up on the subject in hand and bring it to an end if control is being lost

- Do not argue, become angry or enter into a debate with the witness

- Never ask a summary question that might give the witness an opportunity to retract or otherwise explain away responses that helped your case earlier in cross examination

- Move your questions from the general to the specific
- Avoid repeating the same question, even in a different form.

Re-examination

If cross examination results in matters that did not arise in the course in examination in chief, the party that originally called the witness can question the witness again to clarify points which are unclear. Fresh evidence is not permitted without the permission of the court.

Common pitfalls:

- Making comments rather than asking questions
- Not asking a proper question but rather making a statement
- Not giving the witness a proper opportunity to answer the question
- Asking questions that are irrelevant
- Not putting your client's case clearly.

Cross examination of experts

Most expert witnesses are jointly instructed by the parties and the starting point is that their evidence is neutral and independent. The fact that a party does not accept the opinion of the expert is not necessarily a reason for the expert to give evidence at a court hearing. The danger in calling an expert to give evidence carries the likelihood of the expert reinforcing his/her opinion should the expert be cross examined. Whilst an expert's opinion will be taken seriously, it is the court and not the expert who decides the case. Experts should be called to give evidence only if their view or opinion is in doubt by the parties or the court. Their evidence can be presented in the form of a written report which forms part of the

Court Bundle. It is only in exceptional circumstances where an expert will give evidence and be cross examined by the parties.

The object of cross examination of an expert witness can include:

- Challenging or limiting the claimed expertise
- Identifying the parts of opinion outside this expertise
- Identifying what documents were reviewed and what was not reviewed
- Challenging the opinion on the basis of insufficient or incorrect information, that the theory is novel, the procedure is unscientific or their confidence level is unjustified
- Modifying the opinion to reduce its impact.

The Court Decision

Before making an order or refusing an application, the Judge or Lay Magistrates hearing the case must state any findings of fact and the reasons for his/her decision. Any party may obtain a transcript of a judgement of the court.

In the case of Lay Magistrates, the Legal Advisor will, in consultation with the Lay Magistrates, draw up the reasons for the court's decision and any findings of fact. When making the decision, the court must announce these findings. A failure to do may result in a rehearing being ordered. When the court has in mind making an order of a kind that is not part of the original application, the parties should be given the opportunity to address the court on this question. Failure to do so could constitute a defect in the proceedings.

Practice Guidance and Standard Orders have been provided to the Family Court, often in the form of templates, to ensure that court orders contain the essential information and directions relating to a particular hearing. Courts are expected to adopt these forms in order to ensure consistency of wording. These orders will usually include recitals as to who attends the hearing and representation, the issues to be determined in the case, a record of any agreement or concessions made during the hearing and the orders made by the court.

Following a final hearing, the court order should set out in full the orders made together with any appropriate recitals. The court will provide copy of the order to the parties following the hearing.

See Chapter Twenty-Seven for more information on this subject.

CHAPTER ELEVEN

REMOTE COURT HEARINGS IN FAMILY PROCEEDINGS

Remote hearings

A remote hearing is one which is held without the people involved attending court in person. Instead they join the hearing by telephone or by video link using their phone or another device such as laptop or tablet. Sometimes the judge will be at home rather than in the court building. Apart from the fact that people are not in the same building, a remote hearing is exactly the same as a hearing where the parties attend to court in person and the process is broadly the same. The court has all the same powers and will expect people to treat it just as seriously as a 'normal' hearing.

Hybrid hearings

A hybrid hearing is a mixture of a remote hearing and a 'normal' hearing. This means that some of the people involved attend the court in person, and some of them join the hearing remotely by video link or phone. A hybrid hearing might happen if one person cannot physically travel to court. This can happen in some family cases where there are several parties involved. In some cases, one party might attend the courtroom (or another building) so they can be in the same room as their solicitor, but still join the actual hearing by video link. There are a number of different combinations depending on the type of case and the particular circumstances.

The remote hearing itself

When court hearings take place in person in a court building, they do not always start on time because judges often allow parties and their lawyers some flexibility to have discussions before going into the courtroom. It could also be that there are several cases listed at the same time. Remote hearings almost always start on time. It is important that any discussions between the parties have taken place before the start time for the hearing, and that they are ready and waiting at the time the hearing is listed.

It often takes a few minutes for everyone to join the hearing.

At the start of the hearing the Judge will explain that the hearing is being recorded and that It is a criminal offence to record the hearing without permission. If the hearing is heard in private, which is the case for most family court hearings, the Judge will check with everyone involved in the case that they are on their own and somewhere private.

The Judge will make sure people take turns in speaking, and will ask those present not to interrupt. It is a good policy for everyone to put themselves on 'mute' except when they are actually talking, so that background noise does not stop people hearing what is being said. The parties should make sure that, if possible, they have the bundle or the most important documents accessible for reference purposes. Judges can and do hear evidence from witnesses at remote hearings, and can make final orders. It will be for the Judge to decide whether it is fair and suitable for a particular hearing to be dealt with remotely and, if not, what the alternative arrangements can be made.

Joining a remote hearing

The parties will be sent joining instructions before the hearing, either by the court or by the solicitor who is organising the connection.

If the hearing is a telephone hearing, this will usually be arranged by the court and they will call the parties so they can take part. It is important to make sure the court has your up-to-date phone number and that the parties are ready to answer the call when it comes in. The parties should ensure their phone or device is charged or connected to power so that it does not run out of battery during the hearing. If the court is unable to reconnect to a party during the hearing, it might continue on without them. If the hearing is a video hearing, it could be run through one of several different platforms.

Devices, apps or software

The basic requirement is a functioning phone with a reliable connection. Even if the hearing is a video hearing, a party can still join by phone, but it is much easier to follow by video. There are a number of different video platforms that can be used to run a remote hearing, but most of them work in a very similar way. With some video platforms, you might be invited to download an app, but if you prefer, most platforms allow you to join through your internet browser. Cloud Video Platform (CVP) is the Court Service's own video platform. It works through a browser and can be used without needing to download an app.

Support during the remote hearings

If a hearing is a family case the parties should be on your own unless the Judge gives you permission for someone else to be with them. A supporter could be a carer, an Independent Domestic Violence Advocate, a social worker or other support / key worker, a family member or friend or a 'McKenzie Friend'. A supporter might be in the same location as a party during the hearing or they might join the hearing from somewhere else. If the hearing is in private, the Judge may ask the supporter to confirm they understand that they must keep things private, before the hearing goes ahead. Anyone who does attend a hearing to support a party they should remain silent throughout.

If possible, any children should be safely occupied, out of earshot and supervised in another room during the hearing. This is particularly important if it is a family matter about them. A party can still ask the judge about a supporter at the start of the hearing if they have not been able to do this in advance of the hearing.

Communications during the hearing

If a party has a solicitor or supporter, discussions about the best way of communicating during a remote hearing should take in advance of the hearing. Normally a party could whisper to their solicitor in the courtroom, but in a remote hearing they could use WhatsApp, or email, or a separate video link or phone call to communicate privately as things happen. On some platforms, it is possible to set up a private 'room' where a party can have private discussions with their solicitor or supporter (a breakout room).

Requests for a face-to-face hearing

If a party considers there is a need for a face-to-face court hearing this should be raised with the court. The judge has to make a decision on a case-by-case basis depending on:

- the nature of the case and the specific hearing
- the particular needs of the people involved
- what is safe and practical.

If a party has a disability that makes a remote hearing impractical or unsuitable, or if there is a need for an adjustment to be made so that a party can participate the party concerned should raise the matter with the court.

Difficulties during the hearing

It is important that the parties understand what is happening during the hearing. If a party is struggling to see, hear or follow, they should let the judge know at the time. They can do this by speaking, putting their hand up or (on some platforms) pressing a button to raise a 'virtual' hand. The judge may ask everyone who is not speaking to mute their microphones. Sometimes people get cut off from a hearing part way through. Usually the people left behind will get a notification telling them a party has gone, so they will either try and rejoin. If the internet connection goes down, it might be possible to join by telephone.

The Court Order

The court will produce an order recording the outcome of the hearing, and will send everyone involved a copy of the order. If there are lawyers involved they will prepare the order for the judge, and the solicitor will send out the order once it has been approved.

Further Information

The Courts and Tribunals Service (HMCTS) have produced a Guide on Joining Court Hearings by Video Call or Phone:

https://assets.publishing.service.gov.uk/government/uploads/system/uploads/attachment_data/file/876566/

HMCTS have also produced a Guide to How to join Cloud Video Platform (CVP) for a video hearing:

https://www.gov.uk/government/publications/how-to-join-a-cloud-video-platform-cvp-hearing/how-to-join-cloud-video-platform-cvp-for-a-video-hearing

CHAPTER TWELVE

FAMILY PROCEDURE RULES (FPR) 2010 AND RECENT CHANGES

The changes to the Family Procedure Rules (FPR) came into force in April 2024 and have a significant impact on how we conduct family law cases in future years.

The Family Procedure Rules govern the procedures used in family courts in England and Wales and were introduced by Statutory Instrument and are effective from 6th April 2011.

Part 7 (Paragraph 75) of the Courts Act 2003 states that "Family Procedure Rules are to be made **by a committee** known as the Family Procedure Rule Committee", and specifies who should be on that committee.

The Family Procedure Rule Committee

The Family Procedure Rule Committee was set up in October 2004 specifically to make the Family Procedure Rules.

The aim is to produce **one** set of simple and simply expressed rules of court for **all** family courts

It might be useful to know a little about this rule making committee

Day-to-day management of the committee's agenda, and the programme of work, which springs from it, is undertaken by the committee secretariat. The secretariat is part of a team of policy officials at the Ministry of Justice tasked with managing the committee's work.

The Committee meets in London about once a month.

The Courts Act 2003 also states, "Family Procedure Rules may modify the rules of evidence as they apply to family proceedings in any court within the scope of the rules".

In other words the rules can be kept under review and amended if the committee feels this is necessary. That is exactly what has happened recently.

The Family Procedure Rules 2010 are split into **36 parts,** together with the Practice Directions, certain Pre-Action Protocols and a complete set of Forms.

They are intended to modernise and standardise family court practice across the High Court, County Court and Magistrates 'Court.

FAMILY PROCEDURE RULES (FPR)

The family court is obliged to follow the Family Procedure Rules. These rules are designed to inform parties and the court as to' what' to do when you have a case in the family court.

The rules are supplemented by Practice Directions.

The Practice Directions will inform you 'how 'to do something at court.

The number of each Practice Direction coincides with the Part of the Rules to which it relates

For example, Part 12 of the Rules deals with proceedings relating to most children cases and Practice Directions 12A to 12P accompany Practice Directions for that Rule.

There is also an extensive set of forms which accompany the Rules.

All these rules are available as a web version. The rules are also available as a hard copy in a book format. The book is often called the **Red Book.**

Summary of the main areas of the FAMILY PROCEDURE RULES

The OVERRIDING OBJECTIVES of the rules are the starting point

- The overriding objective of the Rules is to enable the court to deal with cases justly, having regard to the welfare issues involved; which means:
- ensuring that the case is dealt with expeditiously and fairly;
- dealing with the case in ways which are proportionate to the nature, importance and complexity of the issues;
- ensuring that the parties are on an equal footing;
- saving expense;
- allotting an appropriate share of the court's resources to the case, while taking into account the response needed to allot resources to other cases.

The court must give effect to the overriding objective when it exercises any of its powers.

The parties are also required to help the court to further the overriding objective.

This means that we all share in the responsibility in achieving these aims

PART 3 – ALTERNATIVE DISPUTE RESOLUTION

It is recognised that an adversarial court process is not always best-suited to the resolution of **family disputes,** especially disputes relating to children.

Therefore, at every stage of the proceedings the court must consider whether alternative dispute resolution (sometimes known as ADR) is appropriate and the court can adjourn the proceedings at any stage in order to enable the parties to engage in ADR.

PART 4 – CASE MANAGEMENT POWERS

Part 4 deals with general case management including the court's general powers of management, the **court officer's** power to refer to the court, the court's power to make an order **of its own initiative** and powers in relation to **sanctions** and reliefs. This will of course include enforcement

PART 5 – FORMS AND START OF PROCEEDINGS

Part 5 deals with the commencement of proceedings and Practice Direction 5A lists the individual forms required for each type of application.

Generally, the forms referred to in a Practice Direction should be used in the cases to which they apply.

Subject to any rule or practice direction, unless the court directs otherwise, a form must have attached to it any documents which the form refers to or states as being required.

Proceedings are started when a court officer **issues** an application at the request of the applicant. The application will be issued on the date entered in the application form by the court officer.

This is useful in cases when there are multiple applications. The date of issue is the guide as to who is the applicant and who is the respondent.

PART 6 – REQUIREMENTS FOR SERVICE

The requirements for service are addressed in Part 6 and by Practice Directions 6A, 6B and 6C. There are various methods of serving documents so clear guidance is very helpful.

The methods of service are outlined at Rule 6.23 which includes service by electronic mail.

PART 12 – CERTAIN PROCEEDINGS WHICH RELATE TO CHILDREN AND THEIR WELFARE

This is really useful for those handling children cases

- **Part 12** deals with proceedings relating to children except parental order proceedings and proceedings for applications in adoption, placement and related proceedings.

- In particular **Part 12** applies to:

- emergency proceedings;

- private law proceedings;

- public law proceedings;

- proceedings relating to the exercise of the court's inherent jurisdiction

- proceedings relating to child abduction and

- proceedings relating to the Council Regulation or the Hague Convention in respect of children.

PART 14 – ADOPTION, PLACEMENT AND RELATED PROCEEDINGS

This is an area less common so an immediate reference point is really helpful.

Part 14 outlines the procedures in relation to applications in adoption, placement and related proceedings.

Details of what needs to be covered in reports on placement and adoption applications are set out in **Practice Direction 14C.**

PART 15 – REPRESENTATION OF PROTECTED PARTIES

Part 15 contains the Rules for dealing with parties **who lack capacity,** known as protected parties.

In particular, the Rules state that a protected party must have a litigation friend to conduct proceedings on that party's behalf.

PART 16 – REPRESENTATION OF CHILDREN AND REPORTS IN PROCEEDINGS INVOLVING CHILDREN

Part 16, along with Practice Direction 16A, covers the representation of children in both private and public law proceedings.

Under Rule 16.2, in non-specified proceedings (e.g. most private law cases or cases involving the exercise of the court's inherent jurisdiction) a child can be made a party to proceedings if the court considers it is in the best interests of the child to do so.

Practice Direction 16A sets out the matters which the court will take into consideration before making a child a party under Rule 16.2.

Rule 16.3 provides for the appointment of a children's guardian in specified proceedings.

PART 17 – STATEMENTS OF TRUTH

Part 17 lists certain documents that must be verified by a statement of truth.

All statements of case, witness statements and applications to the court **must** contain a statement by the parties that they believe the facts they have set out are true.

The consequence of **not** including a statement of truth in a statement of case is that a party who adduces it cannot rely upon its content and the court may strike it out.

In addition, the consequence of **not** including a statement of truth in a witness statement is that the court may direct that it_shall not be admissible as evidence.

The form or wording of a statement of truth is set out in Practice Directive 17A.

PART 22 – EVIDENCE

Part 22 sets out the powers of the court to control the way in which evidence is given.

Rule 22.1 expressly states that the court may control the evidence by giving directions as to:

- the issues on which it requires evidence;
- the nature of the evidence which it requires to decide those issues; and
- the way in which the evidence is to be placed before the court.

PART 27 – COURT BUNDLES

This section details the content, format and timetable of the bundle, including who has responsibility in preparing the bundle.

From a practical point of view, this is a **vital piece** of information.

Anyone undertaking advocacy in a court room will tell you how important it is to get their bundles in the correct form.

PART 30 – APPEALS

Part 30 along with Practice Direction 30A, deals with appeals.

The general time limit for serving notice of appeal is 21 days after the date of the decision which is being appealed.

If the appeal is against a case management decision or an interim care order under section 38(1) of the Children Act, then notice of appeal must be filed within 7 days starting on the date of the decision which is being appealed.

Recent Changes

The Family Procedure Rules have now been updated and, amongst other things, make several changes to improve the level of attendance at mediator initial assessment meetings (known commonly as MIAM) by applicants to certain family proceedings.

These include both financial and children applications

The changes have been introduced because the previous rules were not applied to the extent expected and did not divert cases from court proceedings to the degree that had been anticipated.

Under what were the current rules, it was a requirement for all prospective applicants to attend a MIAM, unless an exemption applies.

These rule changes arise from a push to help more parties settle their cases outside of court.

The Family Procedure (Amendment No. 2) Rules 2023, which came into force in April 2024, amend the Family Procedure Rules 2010.

Rules 2 and 4 came into force on 8 April 2024, and rule 3 and rules 5 to 19 came into force on 29 April 2024.

Key changes in the Family Procedure Rules

The **first change** is a new definition called **Informative requirement.**

The definition included in the rules not only widens the scope for non-court dispute resolution, but also amends rule 3.9(2), which mandates MIAM providers to inform their clients about suitable forms of non-court dispute resolution and provide comprehensive materials on each option.

This requirement ensures that parties are well-informed about all the available alternatives to court proceedings.

The options are likely to include:

- Mediation – including hybrid, shuttle, child-inclusive, and online
- Arbitration

The **second change** is a broader definition of **domestic abuse.**

The definition of "domestic violence" within the FPR has been broadened to "domestic abuse," aligning with the provisions of the **Domestic Abuse Act 2021**.

Furthermore, Rule 3.8(1)(c)(ii) now considers "**significant** financial hardship" instead of "**unreasonable** hardship" in cases involving domestic abuse.

There will still be an exemption where there has been domestic abuse and allow parties to advance straight to court proceedings.

The **third change** is the ongoing consideration of non-court resolution.

This is perhaps the most significant change in that parties are now obligated to consider non-court dispute resolution not only before initiating a case but also throughout its duration.

Rule 3.3(1A) requires parties to file a form with the court and serve it on all parties, expressing their views on non-court dispute resolution.

This ensures continuous evaluation of alternative methods to resolve issues and reinforces the duty on Judges to continue to question if alternative methods should be tried throughout the case.

This also helps the court to understand the parties 'views and question why a party may be opposed to alternative methods without good reason.

There is no doubt that the changes are being implemented so that court users, Judges and lawyers have mediation and other non-court dispute resolution at the forefront of their minds when considering the court, as a means to resolve disputes.

While the practical implementation of these changes remains to be seen, initiatives such as the Pathfinder Pilot in North Wales and judicial endorsements of non-court dispute resolution, as seen in the case of **X vs Y [2024] EWHC 538 (FAM),** where Mrs Justice Knowles endorsed the use of non-court dispute resolution, referring specifically to the new rules, provide promising indications for the future.

The **fourth change** is the removal of agreement requirement.

Previously, cases could be adjourned if parties agreed to consider non-court dispute resolution.

However, this requirement is deleted from the 29 April and an amended rule, Rule 3.4 (1A) will exist.

This rule allows the court to adjourn proceedings to facilitate non-court resolution where "timetabling of proceedings allows sufficient time for these steps to be taken" without explicit agreement from the parties.

What is not clear is whether the parties can be forced to attend.

However, if the parties fail to attend, rule 28.3(7) is now amended to state that failure to engage without good reason may lead to a departure from "no order as to costs".

It is not clear what a "good reason" is and at what stage could a court pause or delay proceedings to consider alternative methods.

This change will almost certainly encourage active participation in alternative methods and will discourage unjustified resistance.

Whilst the new rules strengthen the court's focus on non-court dispute resolution they don't go as far as making it compulsory.

Costs

The general rule as to how costs are treated in financial remedy proceedings is that, usually, each party is to bear their own costs, although it is in the court's power to order one party to pay the other party's costs where it considers it appropriate to do so as a result of their conduct. The scope of such conduct is to be expanded to include failure, without good reason, to attend non-court dispute resolution. Parties embarking on court proceedings will need to be alive to this costs risk if they have not reasonably engaged in other dispute resolution methods.

RECENT CASE LAW

The case of **NA v LA [2024] EWFC 113** considered the court's duty to further the overriding objective by actively case managing has been given added impetus by the revisions to FPR Part 3 and Part 28 which came into effect on the 29 April 2024.

The case itself involved a financial application but many of the comments made within the case, in the author's opinion, could equally apply to a private children case.

On 23 May 2024 Nicolas Allen KC sitting as a Deputy High Court Judge in ***NA v LA***, demonstrated a hands-on approach whilst exercising the powers under the new rules. He considered this a "paradigm case" for the court to exercise its new powers to encourage the parties to engage in Non- court Dispute Resolution ("NCDR") as "*this would be to their emotional and financial benefit as well as the benefit of their children*" and he imposed a stay on the proceedings.

He referred to the ruling of Gwynneth Knowles J in **X v Y (Financial Remedy: Non-Court Dispute Resolution) [2024] EWHC 538** which pre-empted the changes in the FPR coming into effect and which was published so as to ensure that those involved in family proceedings "understand the court's expectation that a serious effort must be made to resolve their differences before they issue court proceedings and, thereafter, at any stage of the proceedings where this might be appropriate" and to signal that "at all stages of the proceedings, the court will be active in considering whether non-court dispute resolution is suitable" and the changes to FPR Part 3 "will give an added impetus to the court's duty in this regard".

The New Rules considered

The judge noted that r 3.4 (1A) (b) provides that where "*the timetabling of proceedings allows sufficient time for these steps to be taken*" the court should "*encourage parties*" to "*undertake non-court dispute resolution*" and that the agreement of the parties to an adjournment for that purpose is no longer required and (at [5]) the court may be give directions about the matters specified in r 3.4 (1A) on the application of a party or of its own initiative (r 3.4 (2)).

And the judge referred to accompanying PD3A which has also been amended with effect from 29 April 2024 and now states *inter alia*:

- at 10A, that while the FPR 2010 does not give the court power to require the parties to attend NCDR, *"the court does have a duty to consider, at every stage in the proceedings, whether non – court dispute resolution is appropriate".*

- at 10 B, that the court *"will want to know the parties' views on using non-court dispute resolution as a way of resolving matters"*; and

- at 10 D, that the court also has general powers to adjourn proceedings (r4.1) which could be exercised to encourage the parties to attend NCDR.

MIAM

The judge held that:

> *"Under r 3.3 (1) the court <u>must</u> consider, at every stage in the proceedings, whether NCDR is appropriate.*
>
> *Under r 3.3 (2) in considering whether NCDR is appropriate the court must take into account:*
>
> - *whether a MIAM took place*
>
> - *whether a valid MIAM exemption was claimed*
>
> - *whether the parties attempted mediation or another form of NCDR and the outcome of the process. there was*

> *nothing in the description of the case that suggest it will be unsuitable for NCDR"*

The judge further noted the amended wording of r 3.10 (1) provides that if a MIAM exemption has been claimed the court will inquire into whether the exemption (a) was not validly claimed; or (b) was validly claimed but no longer applicable.

He observed the judgement of Sir Geoffrey Vos MR in ***Re K* [2022] 2 FLR 1064** at [35] that *"it is a matter of concern that a party can avoid the statutory MIAM requirement by simply asserting that a case is urgent and they need a without notice hearing .... for the statutory MIAM requirement to be effective, it must be enforced."*

Given the terms of the agreed orders the MIAM exemption in this case was no longer applicable.

CHAPTER THIRTEEN

DIVORCE PROCEEDINGS

A client is able to obtain a divorce in England and Wales if he/she:

- has been married for at least one year;
- their marriage is legally recognised by UK law; and
- the relationship has permanently broken down

Usually, one or both parties should be domiciled or resident in England and Wales, but even if that is not the case, the client may still be entitled to divorce here.

As of 6th April 2022, the 'no-fault' divorce laws are in effect. The rules are set out in the Family Procedure (Amendment) Rules 2022.

Under the Divorce, Dissolution and Separation Act 2020:

- Allows joint applications for divorce, civil partnership dissolution and judicial separation. Applicants can still apply on their own (a sole application).
- Ends the need to state one of the five facts or 'grounds' for divorce – adultery, behaviour, desertion, living apart for two or five years.
- Introduces a single requirement for a statement of 'irretrievable breakdown' of the relationship.
- Requires the respondent to a sole application to respond within 14 days.

- Removes the respondent's ability to dispute (formerly defend or contest) the divorce or dissolution.
- Only allows disputed divorce/dissolution on grounds of jurisdiction, validity of the marriage/partnership, or fraud and procedural non-compliance.
- Introduces a new minimum period of 20 weeks between the divorce application being issued and being able to apply for the conditional order (which replaces decree nisi).
- Does not change the current requirement of six weeks and one day between the conditional order and final order (previously decree absolute).
- One party can still apply for a divorce on their own if your spouse does not agree to the divorce or will not cooperate or respond to the court.

The Court Process

For those who are eligible to get a divorce in the UK, the process in England and Wales is as follows:

1. **Application**: Complete **a D8 application form** requesting a divorce or civil partnership dissolution. This can either be on a paper form sent by post or via the Gov.UK digital service online. Parties can apply themselves as a litigant in person or they can appoint a solicitor to act on their behalf.
2. **Sole or joint application:** The applicant will be asked whether the application is being made solely or jointly (with the full knowledge and participation of the spouse/civil partner). In a sole application, there will be an applicant and respondent. In a joint

application, one party will be applicant 1 and the other will be applicant 2.

3. **Personal details:** As a sole applicant he/she will need to complete the details about themselves and the respondent. There is an option to keep the details confidential so that the respondent is not able to view his/her address and phone numbers, etc. On a joint application, both parties must fill in their own details.

4. **Details of the marriage:** There is a requirement to provide the marriage certificate or civil partnership certificate.

5. **Jurisdiction:** There is a need to prove that the parties are eligible to be divorced in England or Wales.

6. **Irretrievable breakdown:** The applicant(s) will need to state that he/she is seeking divorce or dissolution because the marriage/civil partnership has broken down irretrievably. This statement alone will enable the court to make the order for divorce or dissolution.

7. **Other matters:** There is a need to tell the court about previous matters relating to the marriage or civil partnership, such as child proceedings or a previous application for divorce/dissolution. There is a need to tell the court of any other orders the applicant(s) wish to apply for in relation to money, property, and/or children

8. **Statement of Truth:** The statement of truth is the completion and signing of the application. In a joint application, applicant 2 will need to sign this as well.

9. **Serving the application:** A sole applicant can choose how they wish the respondent to receive the divorce application. The default method will be via email or by post if the respondent's email address is not known. If the applicant does not know the address of the respondent, he/she will need to complete form

D11 which enables service via email alone. The applicant can arrange service of the application themselves

10. **Responding to an application:** Respondents to a sole application have 14 days to respond. They will complete a **D10 form.** Disputes on the grounds on grounds of jurisdiction, validity of the marriage/partnership, fraud or procedural non-compliance must be made on form D8B and submitted within 21 days of receiving the divorce/dissolution application.

11. **Apply for the Conditional Order:** After a minimum period of 20 weeks, the sole applicant can apply for the Conditional Order (formerly the decree nisi). Joint applicants must also wait 20 weeks. This period of time can be used to help the parties reflect on whether ending their relationship is the right course of action and also provides time for the parties to attempt to work out other issues such as arrangements for children and finances.

12. **Apply for the Final Order:** Once the Conditional Order has been granted, applicants, either solely or jointly, will need to wait six weeks and one day before they can apply for the Final Order. In sole applications, a 'notice of intention' must be served on the other party 14 days before the application for the Final Order is made.

13. **Granting of the Final Order:** Once the Final Order has been granted the marriage/civil partnership is officially dissolved and legal responsibility for the other party is at an end.

14. **The Court Fee** for divorce is currently £593 but this will increase over time.

CHAPTER FOURTEEN

FINANCIAL APPLICATIONS FOLLOWING DIVORCE

Family Courts have a wide range of powers to make financial orders, including the provision of periodical payments, lump sums, pension sharing, pension attachments, property adjustment, transfer and settlement of property, and a variation of settlements that have already been made.

In the majority of financial cases there are three stages to the court process:

1. The First Directions Appointment (FDA)

This is the first short hearing before a Judge. It usually lasts around 30 minutes. The aim is to make sure that both parties have provided all the information the court needs to decide the value of the matrimonial assets both together and separately. The Judge can do a number of things at the FDA:

- Give directions about what needs to be done before a Judge can decide the case

- Decide which questions on any questionnaire the parties should each answer

- Decide whether the case needs the help of an expert to value an asset the parties cannot agree on, such as the family home or pension

- If the parties agree, make a final order

- Adjourn the proceedings for Mediation
- Treat the First Appointment as a Financial Dispute Resolution Appointment and indicate what order the court might make if the case goes on to a final hearing
- Fix a date for a Financial Dispute Resolution appointment

Advocates at the FDA should ensure the court has all the necessary information to make an order and explore the possibility of a settlement. If a settlement is reached, the advocate for the applicant will draft an order for consideration by the Judge.

Between the FDA and the next hearing

After the First Appointment, the parties should complete all tasks directed by the Judge at the First Directions Appointment by the deadlines given. This may include completing answers to each other's questionnaires, sending these answers to the court and a copy to each other and obtaining an expert's report on the value of the family home or a pension.

If the parties cannot reach an agreement, the court will expect them to make a proposal for settling their case before the Financial Dispute Resolution Appointment. The applicant should write to the court in advance of this hearing taking place, setting out what proposals he/she has made for reaching an agreement and what response has been received. If a party refuses to negotiate, the court can order him/her to pay some of the other party's legal costs.

2. Financial Dispute Resolution Hearing (FDR)

This is the second hearing. At this hearing the court is given a summary of each party's financial position and the District Judge is expected to give an indication as to what he/she believes the outcome should be if the case proceeds to a full hearing. The purpose of this is to allow for the parties to negotiate and reach an agreement. The court will not go into the finer details of the case but will focus on the 'big picture'. The court cannot make a final order at this hearing unless the parties arrive at an agreement between themselves. The parties will be given some time during the course of the day to discuss the Judge's indication to see if an agreement is possible. The Judge who sits at this hearing is not allowed to hear the final hearing. If the parties arrive at an agreement the Judge can make a consent order. If the parties cannot reach an agreement at this hearing, the court will usually give directions for a Final Hearing.

Advocates at the FDR will be expected to make oral submissions on behalf of their client before the Judge gives his/her indication. If the parties are able to arrive at a settlement, the applicant's advocate will draft an order for approval by the Judge. If the parties cannot agree the terms of an order, the court will give directions for the final hearing and advocates will need to make representations to the Judge as to the nature of those directions for example, when the final hearing will take place, what witnesses will give evidence, and who will prepare the court bundle.

3. The Final Hearing

At the Final Hearing the court will hear evidence from both parties and make a final decision as to the outcome. The Judge listens to the evidence, hears speeches from both parties and decides what order should be made as to how the family assets should be divided. These orders are set out in a written court order and presented to the parties. Advocates at the Final hearing will be expected to present evidence, cross examine witnesses and make submissions to the court on behalf of their client. They will also advise the client on a possible appeal and, if necessary, seek the court's permission to appeal.

Consent Orders in Financial Applications

Parties can reach an agreement on financial matters amicably, and so can sign a Consent Order. Even if court proceedings have started, those involved can negotiate and reach an agreement, rather than the court having to make a decision on their behalf. This agreement can then be drafted into a Consent Order.

The court will expect there to have been full and frank disclosure of each party's financial circumstances. This information is set out within a Statement of Information which is sent to the court with a Consent Order. When considering a Consent Order, the court will look at whether the agreement reached is fair, and that there is appropriate financial provision for those involved. The court therefore has a discretionary approach, and does not have to endorse the Consent Order, even if it is agreed by both sides. If both parties have obtained independent legal advice, provided there is evidence of their financial circumstances and the proposed financial settlement is reasonable, it's likely that the Consent Order will be approved by the Judge.

The Consent Order itself can incorporate a number of sections:

- Recitals – agreements that have been reached between the parties which the court cannot order, but should be recorded on the Consent Order to provide clarification.

- Undertakings – promises that are made to the court, that if breached can be enforced by the court. These have to be signed by the person they apply to.

- Orders – these will include orders about property, money and pensions.

The basis of a Consent Order is often to cut the financial ties that spouses and civil partners have with each other. This will prevent either party making further claims in the future. This is known as a Clean Break Order. Once a consent order is approved by the court, it is very difficult to argue that the agreement reached is not appropriate or fair.

Requirements for a Consent Order

In order to approve a Consent Order without a contested hearing, the court requires certain information. This enables the court to make a Consent Order without full investigation and oral evidence. This information is prescribed in Rule 9.26 of the Family Procedure Rules 2010.

(a) The applicant files: Form A Notice of Intention to Proceed with an application for a Financial Order; two copies of a draft of the order sought, one copy endorsed with a statement signed by the respondent to the application signifying agreement. Each party must file with the court and serve on the other party a Statement of Information (Form M (D81)). Where each party's Statement of Information is contained in one form, it must be signed by both the applicant and the respondent to certify that they have read the contents of the other party's statement. Where each party's Statement of Information is in a separate form, the form of each party must be signed by the other party to certify that they have read the contents of the statement contained in that form. A court fee is payable on the filing of the application.

(b) Unless the court directs otherwise, the applicant and the respondent need not attend the hearing of an application for a Consent Order. Where all or any of the parties attend the hearing of a financial application, the court may dispense with the filing of a Statement of Information. If the Consent order is to vary periodical payments or for interim periodical payments, only information as to net income will be required. However, some District Judges may require information about capital at the time of the variation of periodical payments.

Court hearings:
Finance

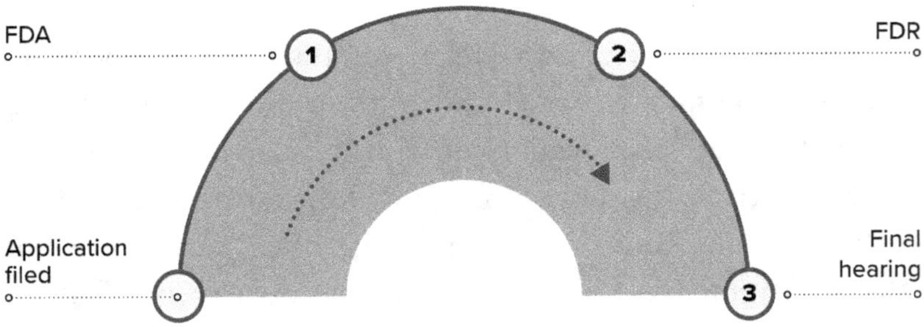

CHAPTER FIFTEEN

PRIVATE CHILDREN APPLICATIONS

Private Law cases are brought by private individuals, generally in connection with divorce or the parents' separation. Orders include: Parental Responsibility, Financial applications, Special Guardianship Orders, and Orders under Section 8 of the Children Act 1989.

Practice Direction 12B The Child Arrangements Programme (CAP) is made up of 23 paragraphs that give a full picture of how the court process should work. See Appendix for details.

The court procedure in Children Act proceedings can vary depending upon the particular application being made and the circumstances of the case, but the most common will be as follows:

1. First Hearing and Dispute Resolution Appointment (FHDRA)

This is the first court hearing after an application has been made to court in private family law proceedings. Form C100 is the usual form of application.

The FHDRA is held to assist the court in identifying issues between the parties at an early stage and to see if it is possible for the parties to reach an agreement. A Cafcass Officer will often be present.

The Judge or Lay Magistrates and the Cafcass Officer will attempt to assist the parties to reach agreement. Sometimes, there will be a Mediator in the court building who might also assist the parties, and if the parties have not yet attempted Mediation, the court may order that they do so before court proceedings commence.

Prior to the hearing, Cafcass should have prepared a Schedule 2 Letter, sometimes known as a Safeguarding Letter, which should be shared with both parties, unless doing so would put either party or the children at risk and/or the document contains information which is sensitive and of which the other party is unaware.

The Schedule 2 Letter will include background checks on the parties. These checks will include enquiries with the Local Authority and the Police as to any relevant information. Cafcass will have spoken to the parties over the telephone to ascertain their views on the application. The Schedule 2 letter usually gives the court guidance as to what steps should be taken to progress the application.

If the parties can reach agreement at the FHDRA, a final order may be made setting out the details of the agreement if the court deems it to be in the children's best interests. If the parties cannot reach agreement, the court will seek to determine the areas where they disagree and the reasons why.

If the case concerns contact and/or residence and serious allegations are made, the court may decide not to permit contact while matters are investigated. The Judge or Lay Magistrates and Cafcass may propose that contact should be supervised or that contact takes place at a Contact Centre while matters are investigated. If there are no serious concerns, the court may order that there should be contact immediately, pending a final order at a future hearing.

Case management decisions considered at the FHDRA include:

- Issues that are agreed and the key issues to be determined
- Whether the matter should be listed for a fact-finding hearing
- Whether any interim orders which can usefully be made e.g. indirect, supported or supervised contact pending a Dispute Resolution Appointment or Final hearing

- What directions are required to ensure the application is ready for a Dispute Resolution Appointment or Final hearing including statements or reports. In particular, whether the court should order a S7 report and the issues to be addressed in the report.

- Whether the application should be listed for a Dispute Resolution Appointment or even a Final Hearing.

Advocates need to prepare carefully for the court hearing and take an active role at the hearing itself. If the parties are able to arrive at an agreement the applicant's advocate will draft an order for approval by the Judge or Lay Magistrates. If the parties cannot agree the terms of an order, the court will give directions for the next hearing. Advocates will need to make representations to the Judge or Lay Magistrates as to the nature of those directions.

2. Dispute Resolution Appointment (DRA)

This is the second hearing when the court will try to narrow the issues in the case, consider any expert evidence (including any S7 report from Cafcass or the Local Authority that has been filed) and decide whether there is a need for a Fact Finding Hearing. Courts use this hearing as an opportunity to resolve matters without the need for a full hearing.

At the DRA the court will:

- identify the key issues to be determined and the extent to which those issues can be resolved or narrowed

- consider whether the DRA can be used as a final hearing

- identify the evidence to be heard on the issues which remain to be resolved at the final hearing

- give final case management directions including:

- filing of further evidence
- filing of a statement of facts/issues remaining to be determined;
- filing of a witness template and/or skeleton arguments
- ensuring compliance with Practice Direction 27A regarding court bundles
- listing the case for a Final Hearing.

No evidence is called at the DRA unless the court has made an earlier direction.

Advocates need to be prepared for the DRA hearing and take an active role in attempting to arrive at an agreement. If the parties are able to arrive at an agreement, the applicants advocate will draft an order for approval by the Judge or Lay Magistrates. If the parties cannot agree the terms of an order, the court will give directions for a Final Hearing. Advocates will need to make representations to the Judge or Lay Magistrates as to the nature of those directions.

3. Fact Finding Hearing

A Fact Finding Hearing is a court hearing that considers the evidence surrounding any serious allegations made by one party against the other. Evidence is heard, which will normally include parties being cross-examined. After having heard the evidence, the Judge or Lay Magistrates will decide whether the alleged incidents happened or not. Most commonly, these allegations concern domestic abuse. Domestic abuse includes neglect, emotional and physical harm and violence. It is for the party making the allegations to prove that they are true. The Judge or Lay Magistrates will consider on the balance of probabilities whether the allegations are true or not.

In preparation for a Fact Finding Hearing the party making the allegations will be asked to provide a list of the allegations to the court in the form of a Scott Schedule. The party against whom the allegations are made will be directed to respond to the allegations within a set time frame. Both parties will be ordered to make written statements setting out their accounts of the allegations. Witnesses can also make a statement and give evidence with the court's permission. The court will often place a limit on the number of allegations to be included in the schedule of allegations to ensure that the case is manageable and the fact finding hearing is focused on the most relevant issues. Advocates will be expected to present their client's case, cross examine witnesses and make submissions to the court. See Chapter 17 for more details on Finding of Fact hearings and in particular the importance of Practice Direction 12J Child Arrangements & Contact Orders: Domestic Abuse and Harm

4. Final Hearing

At a Final Hearing, the Judge or Lay Magistrates will consider all of the evidence of the parties and any Cafcass or Local Authority report. If there has been a Fact Finding hearing the Judge will take into account any findings made in the course of those proceedings. Using all of this information, the Judge or Lay Magistrates will assess the evidence and come to a decision guided by the Welfare Check List. Advocates will be expected to present the client's case, cross examine witnesses and make submissions to the court. The applicant will have prepared a Court

Bundle, agreed the content with the respondent and filed copies with the court.

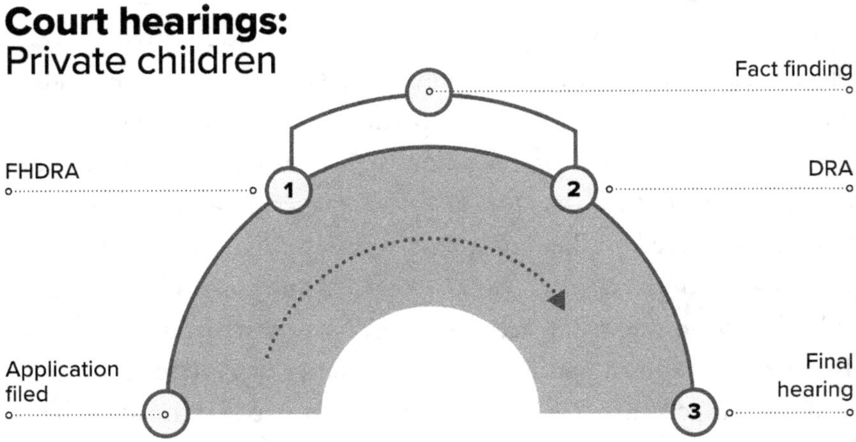

CHAPTER SIXTEEN

PUBLIC LAW CHILDREN APPLICATIONS

Public Law cases are brought by Local Authorities or an authorised person (currently only the NSPCC) where an application is made for a Care Order or Supervision Order in respect of a child. If Social Services believe a child is at risk of significant harm, they can apply to court for permission to take action to protect the child. This will give parental responsibility for the child concerned to the Local Authority applying for the Care order. The Local Authority can also apply for a Supervision Order which places the child under the Supervision of the Local Authority. An Emergency Protection Order is a further order which is used to ensure the immediate safety of a child by taking him/her to a place of safety, or by preventing their removal from a place of safety. Many hearings take place at short notice and involve the advocate in negotiations, submissions and even cross examination at an early stage in the proceedings.

In proceedings under Section 31 of the Children Act 1989 the child's parents and anyone else who holds parental responsibility for the child will be a party to the proceedings. They have a right to attend each court hearing and to have access to all reports and evidence filed with the court. They also have the right to legal representation paid for by legal aid free of any charge.

Practice Direction 12A describes the court process in cases of public law care proceedings.

Section 14(2) of the Children and Families Act 2014 amended s.32(1)(a) of the Children Act 1989 to insert that a case must be concluded without delay and, in any event, within 26 weeks, beginning with the day on which the application was issued.

Interim Care Orders

If Children's Services are of the view that a child needs to be removed from the care of the parents before the final hearing, the social worker in the case will seek an Interim Care Order. The parties in the proceedings will be requested to attend a court hearing to put forward representations.

At this court hearing the court will decide:

- Whether to grant an Interim Care Order
- With whom the child should live with until the final hearing
- Who will have contact with the child until the final hearing

If the court agrees, the Local Authority can take the child into care on a temporary basis initially for up to 8 weeks. This can be extended by permission of the court.

Case Management Hearings

The Case Management Hearing is a court hearing where directions will be made as to how to progress the proceedings. The court gives detailed Case Management directions, including:

- Identifying the key issues
- Identifying the evidence necessary to enable the court to resolve the key issues
- Deciding whether there is a real issue as to threshold to be resolved

This is generally a short hearing which will resolve procedural matters which enables the case to be ready for a final hearing.

Advocates for all parties will work together to bring about an agreement or prepare directions as to any future hearing. A draft order should be prepared, usually by the Local Authority, for the court to consider and approve.

Issues Resolution Hearings

The purpose of this hearing is to decide on whether the care proceedings can be concluded early. If this is not possible, the hearing will identify and narrow down the issues for determination at a final hearing:

- The court identifies the key issues to be determined and the extent to which those issues can be resolved or narrowed down at the IRH.
- The court considers whether the IRH can be used as a final hearing.
- The court resolves or narrows the issues by hearing evidence.
- The court identifies the evidence to be heard on the issues which remain to be resolved at the final hearing.
- The court gives final case management directions.

Advocates will work together to bring about an agreement or prepare directions as to any future hearing. A draft order should be prepared, usually by the Local Authority, for the court to consider and approve.

Final Hearings

If the child's parents, the Children's Guardian and the child's social workers are unable to agree a plan regarding the child, the case will proceed to a final hearing. The court will determine whether a Care Order or a Supervision Order is required to safeguard the welfare of the child. If the court agrees that a court order is necessary given the circumstances, final decisions will be made regarding with whom the child will live and contact arrangements for the parents and wider family.

There are several possible final orders the court can make:

- Care Order: Local Authority gain parental responsibility for the child and the child becomes looked-after until the age of 18 unless discharged before.

- Supervision Order: Local Authority is granted the power to monitor the child's needs whilst the child lives at home or elsewhere.

- Special Guardianship Order: An order that places a child or young person to live with someone other than their parent on a long-term basis.

- Placement Order: The court provide permission to the Local Authority to place a child for adoption even if the child's parents do not provide consent. Most parties, including the child, in care proceedings will be legally represented by an experienced advocate.

Advocates should ensure that their client's case is put to the court at each stage of the proceedings including the court hearings. Negotiations and discussions frequently take place between the parties at and between each court hearing in an attempt to agree legal and procedural issues. In the event of a dispute on such matters, the court will be asked to adjudicate on the issues following representations by all the party's advocates. Parties are not usually expected to give evidence until the final hearing and only if the proceedings are contested. The court may hear evidence from experts, social workers, the Children's Guardian.

CHAPTER SEVENTEEN

DOMESTIC ABUSE INJUNCTIONS

There are two main types of injunctions under Part IV Family Law Act 1996: A Non-molestation Order and an Occupation Order.

Non-molestation Order

This Order aims to prevent a current or former partner/spouse from threatening or using violence against an applicant or a child. The order also aims to stop any harassing or intimidating behaviour. Its ultimate purpose is to protect the health, safety and well-being of the applicant, as well as that of their children.

To apply for an injunction, the applicant must be an 'associated person'. This means the applicant and respondent must be connected with each other in at least one of the following ways:

- they are or were married to each other
- they are or were in a civil partnership
- they live with each other or used to live together
- they live or used to live in the same household
- they are blood relations
- they are engaged to be married to each other even if the engagement ends

- they have children together – this may include those who are parents of the same child, as well as those who have parental responsibility for the same child

- they are in an 'intimate relationship of significant duration'

- they are both taking part in the same family proceedings e.g. children or divorce.

The Domestic Violence Crime and Victims Act 2004 amended the Family Law Act to include same sex couples. This means that people who live together are able to apply for Occupation Orders and Non-molestation Orders, regardless of gender or sexual orientation.

An Occupation Order

An Occupation Order deals with issues as to who lives at the family home and can:

- order the abuser to move out of the home or to stay away from the home

- order the abuser to keep a certain distance away from the home

- order the abuser to stay in certain parts of the home at certain times, for example it can order him/her to sleep in a different bedroom

- order the abuser to allow the applicant back into the home if he/her has locked the applicant out

- order him/her to continue to pay the mortgage, rent or bills

When deciding whether to grant an Occupation Order the court will consider a number of factors including:

- the housing needs and resources of the applicant, the abuser and any children
- the financial resources of the parties
- the likely effect any order, or not making an order, will have on the applicant, the abuser and any child
- the applicant and the abuser's behaviour to one another

The court may also look at the harm that the applicant and any children might suffer if the order is not granted and the harm that the abuser and any child might suffer if an order is made.

The court can make both a Non-molestation Order and an Occupation Order if the court considers it is appropriate.

Those who can be protected by an injunction include the applicant and any relevant child. A relevant child is any child under 18:

- who is living or might be expected to live with the applicant or the abuser
- who is the subject of Family Court proceedings linked to an application for a Domestic Violence injunction; or
- whose interests the court thinks relevant

- If the child is over 18, or another adult family member needs protection, they will have to make their own application for an injunction.

Court hearings:
Injunctions

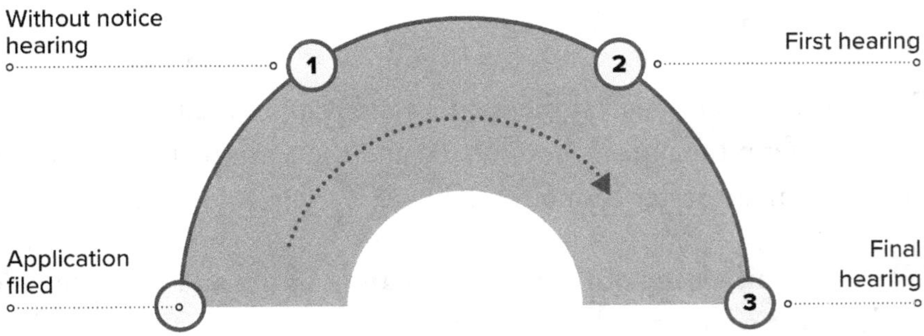

The application process

An application for a Non-molestation Order and/or an Occupation Order is made in the Family Court. The application form is FL401. There is no court fee for applying for a Domestic Violence Injunction. A witness statement should be filed giving details of the applicant's relationship with the respondent, any relevant children, past history of violence and the events which led to the making of an application and the order being sought.

Without Notice Hearing

If the injunction is urgent or the abuser could cause further harm if he/she is aware of the court application, the application can be made without notice to the respondent. In this case, the court can consider the application without the respondent being served or present at court. The court will have to be persuaded that there are good reasons to make an order urgently and in the absence of the respondent, which should be set out in the witness statement. Supporting documents from the Police or a doctor can help and should be attached as an exhibit to the witness statement.

If an order is granted without notice to the respondent, the court will set another hearing date to give the respondent an opportunity to put forward his/her response to the application.

The applicant will have to attend this hearing and may have to give evidence. The court will consider all the evidence and decide whether the order should be extended or varied.

As an alternative to an Order, the court may accept an Undertaking from the respondent. An Undertaking is a binding promise which the respondent makes to the court. It can be offered in lieu of a court order. In domestic abuse proceedings, an Undertaking is a promise to do or to avoid all the steps contemplated by the proposed court order. This means that the respondent agrees to observe these stipulations, but it is not a court order. Although an Undertaking is not a court order, it is still enforceable.

If respondent fails to honour his/her promise, then the applicant can seek to commit the respondent to prison for contempt of court. This is done by lodging an application for committal to prison, with an affidavit, listing details of the breach.

If the court is satisfied the respondent has breached the Undertaking, it can deal with the matter by imposing:

a) Imprisonment for up to 2 years

b) Suspended sentence of imprisonment

c) An unlimited fine.

An Undertaking can only be made with the consent of the respondent.

An Undertaking should only be offered if he/she has genuinely behaved in a sufficiently threatening or unreasonable fashion. This does not mean that the respondent has to accept all the matters alleged against him/her but can be based on the respondent's own version of events. It is important that the respondent does not to agree to an Undertaking simply to avoid the case proceeding to a full hearing. The respondent should agree an Undertaking only in circumstances when the respondent admits behaviour that might otherwise merit a court order being made against him/her.

The major difference between an Undertaking and a Court Order lies in enforcement of breach:

a) In the case of a breach of a Non-molestation Undertaking, it gives rise to Contempt of Court Enforcement Proceedings, whereas with a breach of a Non-molestation Court Order it is a criminal offence, and if proved will result in a criminal penalty and criminal record.

b) An Occupation Order can have attached to it a power of arrest, so a party breaching it can be arrested and brought to court in custody.

An Occupation Undertaking cannot have a power of arrest attached so the applicant will have to apply to court for a warrant for the respondent's committal.

The advantage of an Undertaking is that an Undertaking is not a Court Order. An Undertaking avoids the risk of criminal penalty for breach, the need for a contested injunction hearing is avoided, and neither party has to give evidence at a trial.

Advocates at these hearings should ensure that their client's case is put to the court at each stage of the proceedings including the court hearings. Negotiations and discussions frequently take place between the parties at the adjourned hearing in order to arrive at an agreement for the making of an order and the terms of such an order. Discussions on the possibility of an Undertaking can take place. In the event of a dispute, the court will be asked to adjudicate on the issues, following representations by all the party's advocates. Parties may be expected to give evidence. Advocates will present their client's case, cross examine witnesses and make submissions to the court.

Service of Court Orders

The applicant is responsible for serving the court order by handing a copy of the order to the respondent. This should usually be undertaken by a Process Server. The respondent must know there is an injunction in place to be responsible for breaching any part of it. The applicant is only protected once the respondent is aware of the order. A copy of the order should also be delivered to the local Police station.

Breach of a Court Order

If the respondent breaches the injunction, the applicant will need to enforce it. If the respondent has breached the Non-molestation Order it can be enforced by either by reporting his behaviour to the Police or commencing civil proceedings by applying to the court that made the order for the respondent to be arrested and/or punished.

Breaching a Non-molestation Order is a criminal offence that can be dealt with by the criminal court. The criminal courts have a range of sentencing options available to them. The maximum sentence is 5 years imprisonment and a fine.

If an Occupation Order is in place, the process for enforcing the order varies depending on whether a power of arrest is attached to the order. A power of arrest allows Police officers to arrest the respondent if the occupation order is breached. A power of arrest can be attached to an Occupation Order if the court is satisfied that the respondent has used or threatened violence against the applicant. If the abuser breaches any part of the Occupation Order and there is a power of arrest attached to it, the applicant can report the breach directly to the police.

The Police can arrest him/her and bring him before the court that made the order to be punished. The court may hear evidence about the breach and deal with the respondent immediately, or the court may adjourn the hearing to another day.

If an Occupation Order does not have a power of arrest attached, the applicant can still apply to the court that made the order to have the abuser arrested and/or punished, if he/she has breached any part of the Order. A respondent who is found by the court to have breached the order may be committed to prison, fined or be given a suspended sentence of imprisonment.

CHAPTER EIGHTEEN

OTHER FAMILY PROCEEDINGS

Harassment

If the applicant is not 'associated' with the abuser, the applicant may still be able to obtain protection if he/she is suffering harassment or being put in fear of violence. The Protection from Harassment Act 1997 makes it a criminal offence to harass someone or make them fear violence will be used against them. The applicant can apply for an Injunction against the person harassing him/her or making him/er fear violence and can also claim damages from him/her.

Definition of harassment

Harassment is a course of conduct that is deliberately intended to cause a person distress or alarm. A course of conduct means two or more incidents of harassment. When deciding whether any particular course of conduct amounts to harassment, the court will consider whether a reasonable person would think that it amounts to harassment.

Examples of harassment could be:

- a text, answer-phone message, letter or email
- a comment or threat
- standing outside someone's house or driving past it
- an act of violence.

Putting someone in fear of violence is a course of conduct that causes another person to fear that violence will be used against them. A person is guilty of putting someone in fear of violence if their behaviour is such that a reasonable person, with the same information, should know that the behaviour would cause them to have that fear.

Protection from harassment and being put in fear of violence

The victim can report an incident of harassment or being put in fear of violence to the police. The Police may give the abuser a warning of the consequences of his behaviour or arrest him for the criminal offences of harassment or putting someone in fear of violence.

The criminal courts can make a Restraining Order if the abuser is found guilty or if he is acquitted of the offence. The Crown Prosecution Service (CPS) can request the Restraining Order which can prohibit an abuser from doing anything specified in the order including using or threatening violence against the victim, communicating by phone or email or going to certain places such as a home or place of work. In addition to or instead of contacting the police, the victim can apply for an injunction under the Protection From Harassment Act 1997. The victim can also ask for damages from the abuser.

Cohabitation

The law treats cohabitants on relationship breakdown as two unrelated individuals. No account is taken of their relationship in terms of financial or other contributions they may have made in order to determine a fair outcome between them on separation or death. This is in spite of many couples being in long-term relationships and/or having children together. Cohabitation does not provide an automatic or guaranteed right to ownership of a partner's property. Cohabitants can apply under Section 14 of the Trusts of Land and Trustees Act 1996 for the court to determine whether or not a party has an interest in a property, the extent of such interest and how that interest is to be realised. The court has no power to override the strict legal ownership of property and divide it as it may do on divorce or dissolution of a civil partnership. Cohabitation disputes can only be determined where rules of Trusts or Proprietary Estoppel apply. In some circumstances, a former cohabitant may apply for an order for financial provision in the form of transfer or settlement of property orders, periodical payments or lump sum orders on behalf of their children under Schedule 1 Children Act 1989. However, this only provides short term relief as orders only continue until a child reaches the age of 18 or ceases full time education.

The surviving cohabitant of a partner who dies without leaving a will, has no automatic right under the intestacy rules to inherit any part of his/her partner's estate. A surviving cohabitant may be able to make a claim under the Inheritance (Provision for Family and Dependants) Act 1975 if no provision or inadequate provision has been made for them either by will or by operation of the intestacy rules, but cohabitants are not treated in the same way as a spouse.

Schedule 1 Children Act 1989

In some circumstances where a couple have children, whether or not they ever lived together, there is an option for making an application to the court for an order under Schedule 1 Children Act 1989 for the following:-

1. Maintenance to be paid for a child if one parent lives abroad, or where the non-resident parent earns more than the maximum amount the CSA or CMS will take into account. The latter are known as "Top Up" orders. The court may also make maintenance orders to pay for educational expenses, a child's disability, or where a child is over the age of 18 and is remaining in education. A child going to University may make an application him/herself.

2. Capital orders. A lump sum or sums may be ordered to be paid nominally for a particular expense e.g. to pay for a family car.

There is no limit on the number of lump sum applications that can be made.

3. A property to be transferred or held in trust for the benefit of a child temporarily usually until a child attains the age of 18 or ceases full time Secondary or University education. At that stage, the property will either be returned to the payer or sold and the proceeds returned to the payer.

Forced Marriages

A number of designated courts have powers to prevent forced marriages, and to offer protection to victims who might have already been forced into a marriage.

Advocates in all the above cases will be expected to present their client's case, cross examine witnesses and make submissions to the court.

CHAPTER NINETEEN

FACT FINDING HEARINGS

Introduction

- If one party makes allegations during family law proceedings and the other party denies those allegations, the court will consider whether there should be a Fact Finding Hearing. This is a separate hearing arranged to decide whether or not the allegations are true. Fact Finding hearings are most common in children cases, but can also take place during other family law proceedings such as for domestic abuse injunctions or financial remedies.

- At the Fact Finding Hearing the court considers the evidence surrounding allegations made by one party against the other and makes a decision as to whether alleged incidents did or did not happen. The parties give evidence in the witness box and are cross-examined. After having heard the evidence, the Judge or Lay Magistrates will decide whether the alleged incidents happened or not. Most commonly, these allegations concern domestic abuse but can relate to other aspects of behaviour. It is for the party making the allegations to prove that they are true. The Judge or Lay Magistrates will consider on the balance of probabilities whether it is more likely than not that the allegations are true.

Reasons for a Fact Finding Hearing

The decision about whether to hold a Fact Finding Hearing is for the court not CAFCASS or the parties. At the first hearing of the private children application (FHDRA) the court has to consider ***Practice***

Direction 12J Child Arrangements & Contact Orders: Domestic Abuse and Harm (**PD12J**), which informs the court how it should approach cases involving allegations of domestic abuse. The thrust of *PD12J* is that if disputed allegations could be potentially relevant to the decision the court is to make about the child, the court should determine the dispute by deciding whether the allegations are true or not. The decision about whether or not to hold a fact finding hearing should generally be taken early.

The purpose of this Practice Direction is to assist the Family Court in its decision making when a party alleges she/he has experienced domestic abuse perpetrated by another party.

The general principles are set out in **Paragraphs 4-8. Practice Direction 12J Practice Direction 12J Child Arrangements & Contact Orders: Domestic Abuse and Harm:**

Paragraph 4 states:

> 'Domestic abuse is harmful to children, and/or puts children at risk of harm, whether they are subjected to domestic abuse, or witness one of their parents being violent or abusive to the other parent, or live in a home in which domestic abuse is perpetrated (even if the child is too young to be conscious of the behaviour). Children may suffer direct physical, psychological and/or emotional harm from living with domestic abuse, and may also suffer harm indirectly where the domestic abuse impairs the parenting capacity of either or both of their parents.'

Paragraph 5 states:

> The court must, at all stages of the proceedings, and specifically at the First Hearing Dispute Resolution Appointment (FHDRA), consider whether domestic abuse is raised as an issue, and if so, act appropriately by:

- identifying the factual and welfare issues involved

- consider the nature of any allegation, admission or evidence of domestic abuse, and the extent to which it would be likely to be relevant in deciding whether to make a child arrangements order and, if so, in what terms

- give directions as appropriate

- ensure that where domestic abuse is admitted or proven, any child arrangements order in place protects the safety and wellbeing of the child <u>and</u> the parent with whom the child is living, and does not expose either of them to the risk of further harm

- ensure that any interim child arrangements order is only made having followed the guidance set out in the practice direction.

Scott Schedule (Paragraph 19c)

- In preparation for a Fact Finding Hearing, the party making the allegations will be directed to serve a list of the allegations in the form of a *Scott Schedule*. The list should be signed and dated, each incident should be numbered and set out in date order stating the date of the incident and details of what happened and where, details of any witnesses to the incident and involvement of the police and/or medical services. The list should contain a statement that it is true. The person against whom the allegations are made will be directed to respond to the allegations. The person accused should respond to each allegation in turn, setting out their account of the incident or stating that the allegation is denied. Both parties will also be asked to make written statements setting out their evidence. Witnesses can also make a statement and give evidence with the court's permission.

- If a party has been directed to serve or respond to a Scott Schedule a template form can be used which includes:
- Heading – as with all of court documents
- Number – number the allegations
- Date – date that the incident or behaviour has occurred. If the behaviour happened on more than one occasion dates can be listed. If the behaviour has taken place over a period of time insert when it started and ended. If the abuse is still taking place state 'Ongoing from (date abuse started) until now.'
- Allegations – keep these short and factual. The details of the incidents will be in the party's statement.
- Reference – state where the details of the allegation are in the court bundle
- Refer to any other supporting evidence, for example from the Police, Local Authority or medical records so that the Judge can easily find all the evidence available
- Response – this section is for the other (accused) party to put their response to each allegation. The party preparing the schedule leaves this part blank for the other party to fill in. They will need to say whether they admit or deny the allegations. If they deny an allegation it means they do not agree that it happened. The person responding to the allegation will also need to refer to any evidence they have provided on the allegation
- Judge's finding – leave a column in the table for the Judge to complete at court. The Judge will hear evidence and decide whether they find each allegation to be true. If the Judge finds that an allegation is true he/she will state that the allegation is

found. If the Judge decides that the allegation is not true he/she will state that the allegation is not found. If the Judge cannot decide whether the allegation is true or not he/she may state that the allegation cannot be determined either way

- Sign, print name and date the schedule

Paragraphs 35–37 Practice Direction 12J set out the procedural framework to be followed. It details factors to be taken into account when determining whether to make Child Arrangements Orders in all cases where domestic abuse has occurred. When deciding the issue of child arrangements, the court should ensure that any order for contact will not expose the child to an unmanageable risk of harm and will be in the best interests of the child.

Paragraphs 38 to 40 Practice Direction 12J provides for directions as to how contact is to progress including indirect contact. The court is required, in its judgment or reasons to make clear how its findings on the issue of domestic abuse have influenced its decision regarding arrangements for the child.

Witness Statements

Each party must prepare a witness statement. Usually the person making the allegations goes first. Each allegation or incident will be dealt with by the parties. Sometimes the court will place a limit on the number of allegations that should be included in the schedule of allegations to ensure that the case is manageable and the Fact Finding Hearing is focused on the most relevant issues.

The Fact Finding Hearing Itself

The general format of a Fact Finding Hearing will be as follows:

- The person making allegations of abuse (and his/her witnesses) will give evidence first. The party will confirm (or correct) their witness statement and may then be asked questions by or on behalf of the other party. Sometimes the Judge will ask some questions.

- The same process then happens for the person who is accused of abuse and any witnesses he/she has brought to court.

- The parties (or their Solicitor if they have one) will then be able to make submissions, to the Judge.

- The Judge will announce the decision and give reasons.

This process might vary if one or both parties has no Solicitor and the court makes special arrangements because of that.

Statutory changes

- The **Domestic Abuse Act 2021** came into force on 29 April 2021. For the family courts, there are several implications, in particular, provision for protection for victims and witnesses in legal proceedings: The prohibition on cross-examination in person by those alleged to be victims or perpetrators of domestic abuse (**section 65 Domestic Abuse Act 2021**).

- This subject is highly relevant in finding of fact hearings. The removal of legal aid for many private family law cases means that one or both parties are unrepresented in a large number of cases. The prohibition of cross-examination is introduced through an amendment to the Matrimonial and Family Proceedings Act 1984 by insertion of 31Q-31Z which came into force on the 21st July 2022.

- Under the **Domestic Abuse Act 2021** there can be prohibition on cross-examination in four circumstances:

- First, there is a prohibition for cross-examination by a party who has been convicted, cautioned, or is charged with a specified offence. It will also prevent victims of domestic abuse (or a specified offence) from having to cross-examine a witness who has been convicted, cautioned or charged with that offence. The specified offences will be defined in the regulation, which is not yet in place.

- Second, there is a prohibition on cross-examination by a party subject to an on-notice protective injunction. This also extends to parties who are protected by an on-notice injunction.

- The third category includes a similar prohibition on cross-examination, but where there is 'specified evidence' of domestic abuse.

- The fourth category is a safety valve where none of the above applies. In the absence of applicability of any of the above, the Court will have the power to prohibit a party from cross-examining a witness in person if:

    - The quality condition or the significant distress condition is met; and

    - It is not contrary to the interest of justice to give the direction.

The quality condition is met if the quality of the evidence is likely to be diminished if cross-examined by the party in person, and the quality of the evidence would be improved if the direction were given under the section.

Where any of the above conditions are met, the Court will consider if there are any alternative means for the witness to be cross-examined.

In cases when the Court considers there is no alternative, the Court must invite the party to the proceedings to arrange for a legal representative and require the party to notify the Court, by the end of a period specified by the Court, whether a legal representative is to act for the party.

If the party has notified that they will not have a legal representative or has not notified at all, then the Court will consider if it is necessary in the interests of justice for the witness to be cross-examined by a Qualified Legal Representative (QLR) appointed by the Court to represent the interest of the party. The Lord Chancellor has made provision for payment to legal representatives to be made out of central funds.

See Chapter Twenty for more details regarding the role of the QLR.

Possible future changes to procedure

Following the cases in the Court of Appeal of **Re H-N and Others (children) (domestic abuse: finding of fact hearings)** [2021] **EWCA Civ 448** the court stated:

> 1. *It is accepted by the court, the parties and within the two reports, that PD12J remains fit for the purpose for which it was designed, namely to provide the courts with a structure enabling the court first to recognise all forms of domestic abuse and thereafter on how to approach such allegations when made in private law proceedings*

2. Specific guidance was given by the court in relation to:

- *Whether there should be a finding of fact hearing*

The proper approach ... emphasises the need to consider the nature of the allegations, the relevance to the decision to be made in relation to the child, and the need for the court to decide if a fact-finding hearing is 'necessary and proportionate';

- *The use of Scott Schedules.*

The court endorsed the view ... that the time has come for there to be a move away from Scott Schedules as a means of identifying issues to be tried by the Family Court. Scott Schedules, which identify specific factual incidents tied to a particular date and time, are at risk of failing to focus on the wider context and whether there has been a pattern of coercive and controlling behaviour;

- *The approach to controlling and coercive behaviour.*

The court emphasised the need to evaluate the existence or otherwise of a pattern of coercive and controlling behaviour without significantly increasing the scale and length of private law proceedings, in circumstances where delay is inimical to the welfare of a child and the courts;

- *The relevance of criminal law concepts*

Whilst the Family Courts and the parties who appear in them should not shy away from using words such as 'rape' in the manner in which they are used in ordinary speech, the law is clear that criminal law concepts should not be imported to the Family court. There is a distinction between judges needing to understand the potential psychological impact of sexual assault on a victim on the one hand and the importance of Family judges avoiding being drawn into an analysis of factual evidence based on criminal law proceedings on the other.

It should be stressed that the guidance given by the Court of Appeal in these cases has no formal legal authority at present but it is likely that changes are likely to be made on these issues in due course.

The case of **AA v BB [2021] EWHC 1822 (Fam)** considered the implications of **Re H-N**. In that case the appeal was against a case management decision to exclude evidence from a fact finding hearing. The mother relied on the dicta of the Court of Appeal in **Re H-N** regarding **the limitations** of Scott Schedules and the fact that the court focused on particular allegations **rather than** looking at patterns of overall behaviour.

The Court of Appeal then heard the case of **K v K [2022] EWCA 468** which states ' This judgement is intended to provide general guidance on the proper approach to fact-finding hearings in private family proceedings following this courts decision in **Re H-N**.

A summary of the principles of **K v K** are these:

(a) the nature of the allegations **and the extent** to which those allegations are likely to to relevant **to the making of the child arrangements order;**

(b) that the purpose of fact finding is to allow **assessment of the risk to the child** and the **impact** of any abuse on the child;

(c) whether fact finding **is necessary** or whether other evidence suffices and;

(d) whether fact finding is **proportionate.**

The court expressed concern that a perception had formed that **Re H-N** created a requirement that in every case in which allegations of domestic abuse are made, the court should conduct a fact finding exercise with a detailed analysis of each specific allegation. The Court of Appeal reiterated that the courts duty is limited to determining determining factual disputes that are likely to be relevant to deciding how to make a child arrangements order.

The emphasis now placed by the Court of Appeal on the relevance and effect of disputed facts was expressed simply at para 45: 'without in anyway resiling from what was said at [139] of ***Re H-N*** about the pernicious nature of domestic abuse, fact-finding is only needed_if the alleged abuse is likely to be relevant to what the court is being asked to decide relating to the children's welfare.

This case sends a signal to family courts to be discerning when deciding on *the need* to have a fact finding hearing.

Other helpful cases include:

- B v B 2022 EWHC 108 (Fam) (Process of clustering)
- Re A (A Child: Findings of Fact) 2022 EWCA Civ 1652
- Re M [2021] EWHC 3225 (Fam) (Vulnerable witnesses)
- D v R [2023] EWHC 406 (Fam)
- A Local Authority v X & Ors (Need for Finding of Fact hearing) 2023 EWFC 121(Whether a Finding of fact hearing is necessary)
- Re E [2019] EWCA Civ 1447 (Test for Reopening Finding of Fact hearing)

CHAPTE TWENTY

QUALIFIED LEGAL REPRESENTATIVES (QLR)

For some time, the judiciary has called for provision of an advocate to ask questions of a vulnerable witness on behalf of a litigant in person. The introduction of a power for courts to appoint a 'Qualified Legal Representative' (QLR) to undertake cross examination is set out in the Domestic Abuse Act 2021

The Prohibition of Cross-examination of Litigants in Person

The coming into force of section 65, Domestic Abuse Act 2021 on the 21st July 2022 saw the introduction of the prohibition on cross-examination in person by parties alleged to be either victims or perpetrators of domestic abuse, as introduced by the insertion of Part 4B, Matrimonial and Family Proceedings Act 1984 (section 31Q – 31Z)

The new provisions meet the concerns expressed by Hayden J as to the practice of litigants in person in family proceedings being able to cross examine their victim in domestic abuse cases, which he described in PS v BP [2018] as 'manifestly irrational and unfair'.

Summary of the changes

Under Part 4B, Matrimonial and Family Proceedings Act 1984, there can be a prohibition on cross-examination in four circumstances:

- where a party has been convicted, cautioned or charged with a specified offence;
- where a party is subject to an on-notice protective injunction;

- where there is 'specified evidence' of domestic abuse; and
- a 'catch all' category, where, in the absence of any of the above, the court has the power to prohibit a party from cross-examining a witness in person if the 'quality condition' or the 'significant distress condition' are met and it is not contrary to the interest of justice to give the direction.

Where any of the above conditions are met, the court will consider whether there are any alternative means for the witness to be cross-examined, or to obtain evidence that the witness might have given under cross-examination.

In cases when the court considers there is no alternative, it must invite the party who would have undertaken cross-examination to arrange for a legal representative and require them to notify the court by the end of a specified period whether a legal representative is to act for them. If the party has notified the court that they will not have a legal representative, or has not notified the court at all, then the court will consider if it is necessary in the interests of justice for the witness to be cross-examined by a qualified legal representative appointed by the court to represent the interests of that party , the court must appoint a legal representative to cross-examine the witness.

Litigants in person

Many private family law cases involve one or both parties being unrepresented by a qualified lawyer.

According to Joint Research by Cafcass and Women's Aid domestic abuse allegations were present in 62% of private law children proceedings. At the same time, there has been a rise in applications for domestic abuse remedy orders such as non-molestation orders or occupation orders. Family courts have struggled to cope with hearings where allegations of domestic abuse have been made against parties who have conducted their own case. In order to address this issue a litigant in person is now obliged to instruct their own lawyer (at their own expense) or accept a lawyer appointed by the court.

The role of a court appointed legal representative

Section 31(W)(7), MFPA1984 makes it clear that the appointed legal representative is not responsible to the party on whose behalf they have been appointed to cross-examine.

The Ministry of Justice has issued statutory guidance about the role of qualified legal representatives appointed by the court. The guidance states (at para 3.3) that:

- the court will make clear to the prohibited party that the qualified legal representative is not their lawyer and that they are appointed by the court only to cross-examine a certain witness or certain witnesses;
- the qualified legal representative must clearly communicate the limited nature of their role and relationship with the prohibited party and that they do not have a contractual relationship with the prohibited party;
- the qualified legal representative must also make it clear that they cannot give advice or represent the prohibited party throughout the case, but are appointed by the court to carry out a very limited role;
- the qualified legal representative cannot help with preparing documentation or assist in complying with directions; and
- the court-appointed qualified legal representative will need to explain to the prohibited party that they cannot promise the confidentiality that usually attaches to lawyer-client relationships (legal professional privilege) and that there are obligations in

family and civil proceedings to disclose material that may be unhelpful to the prohibited party's case.

The statutory guidance advises (at para 1.1):

> Whilst the qualified legal representative appointed by the court must have regard to this guidance, the guidance does not seek to restrict the exercise of the qualified legal representative's professional judgment. However, it does set out principles and limitations which are distinctive to this statutory role and which must be reflected in the qualified legal representative's actions and decisions.

How it works in practice?

The guidance issued to the qualified legal representative sets out some significant restrictions on the nature and extent of their role in acting for the prohibited party: The qualified legal representative is not their lawyer; they do not have a contractual relationship ; they cannot give advice or represent the prohibited party throughout the case; they cannot help with preparing documentation or assist in complying with directions; they cannot promise confidentiality and there are obligations in family proceedings to disclose material that may be unhelpful to the prohibited party's case. Yet, at the same time, it is said that the guidance does not seek to restrict the exercise of the qualified legal representative's professional judgment.

Procedure and points to note

- The court makes a decision that a party (a Litigant in Person) is prohibited from cross examining an opponent.

- The court will make an order for a QLR to be appointed to cross examine on behalf of the prohibited party.

- The court sends out an invitation to the QLRs on the court list.
- Once a QLR has been identified, an order is made for that particular advocate to be appointed.
- The QLR will receive the court bundle to prepare for the hearing.
- He/she will attend court, meet the Litigant in Person in question and discuss what matters need to be addressed by way of cross examination.
- It is important to note that the QLR does not act for the Litigant in Person generally.
- There is, for example, no duty to make submissions.
- There is no solicitor and client relationship.
- Once the exercise of cross examination has taken place the QLR will usually leave the court room and play no further part in the proceedings.
- The final court order will set out details of what work has been undertaken by the QLR.
- The fees of the QLR are paid from Central Funds via the Legal Aid Agency.

Shortage of QLRs

Re Z (prohibition on Cross Examination: No QLR) [2024] EWFC 22

Within his judgment, Sir Andrew McFarlane reminds us of the QLR process, guidance and, most importantly, the issue many judges and magistrates are currently facing on a daily basis – what to do when a QLR is required but none is available?

Key points to take away from this judgment include:

- Cases should not be permitted to drift; when directing the appointment of a QLR, a requirement should be included in the court's order directing that the case be returned to the judge/justices for further directions if, after 28 days (or whatever reasonable period is chosen), the court has not succeeded in appointing the QLR. The principal options facing a court at the directions hearing are likely to be:
    - A further adjournment in the hope that a QLR may be found;
    - An adjournment to allow one or both parties to engage their own advocate;
    - Reviewing the need for the vulnerable party to give oral evidence and be cross-examined. This will include reviewing the need for there to be a fact-finding hearing in the proceedings;
    - Considering any other alternative means of avoiding in person cross-examination between the relevant parties;
    - The court itself taking on the task of asking questions in place of the in person party.
- It does not follow that, if no QLR is available, the court is automatically required to conduct the questioning itself. It is important that all possible alternative options are reviewed at that point in the proceedings.

- The court should take account of PD3AB paragraph 5.3 <u>BUT</u> PD3AB, paragraph 5.3 is not, however, black-letter law. The fact that the PD does not include questioning by the court as a satisfactory alternative, does not, as a matter of law, prevent the court undertaking the task if it considers that, in the interests of justice, it must nevertheless do so.

- In the context of a decision on how to proceed in the absence of a QLR, FPR 2010 r1.1(2)(a), (b) and (c) are likely to be of particular relevance.

- The need to ensure that the parties are on an equal footing coupled with the need to bring the proceedings to an expeditious and fair conclusion in a proportionate manner, is likely to lead a court to conclude that there is no other alternative but for it to ask the necessary questions.

- If the court decides to abandon further attempts to appoint a QLR, the previous direction appointing one must be discharged and the reasons for discharge should be very shortly recorded on the face of the order and/or in a short judgment.

- Where a judge is required to ask questions on behalf of one or both parties, he or she must guard all the more against being drawn into the arena so as to lose objectivity and diminishing their ability properly to evaluate and weigh the evidence.

- A further need for caution may arise from the need for the judge to avoid taking an important point on behalf of one party which that party has not, themselves, raised (see Villiers v Villiers [2022] EWCA Civ 722 at paragraph 212). During a fact-finding hearing, it must be expected that a judge may spot a point that has not been raised by either party, but requires clarification. In such circumstances, provided that the manner in which the judge raises the point and questions the party or parties about it is fair, judges should not feel that they are prevented from doing so.

- In every case fairness requires the court to be very open with the parties as to the process that is going to be adopted by explaining what is to happen, step by step, at the start in short straight forward terms.

- The court should explain that it is taking on the role of asking questions in order for the hearing to proceed in the absence of a QLR, and where there is no other satisfactory alternative – courts should refer to it as the court 'asking questions that the other party wishes to have asked', or a similar phrase (rather than using the phrase 'cross-examination').

- Sir Andrew McFarlane agreed with the approach of Hayden J in PS v BP [2018] EWHC 1987 (Fam):

    - Once it becomes clear to the court that it is required to hear a case "put" to a key factual witness where the allegations are serious and intimate and where the witnesses are themselves the accused and accuser, a "Ground Rules Hearing" (GRH) will always be necessary;

    - The GRH should, in most cases, be conducted prior to the hearing of the factual dispute;

    - Judicial continuity between the GRH and the substantive hearing is to be regarded as essential;

    - It must be borne in mind throughout that the accuser bears the burden of establishing the truth of the allegations. The investigative process in the court room, however painful, must ensure fairness to both sides. The Judge must remind himself, at all stages, that this obligation may not be compromised in response to a witnesses' distress;

- Where the factual conclusions are likely to have an impact on the arrangements for and welfare of a child or children, the court should consider joining the child as a party and securing representation. Where that is achieved, the child's advocate may be best placed to undertake the cross-examination.

- If the court has decided that cross-examination will not be permitted by the accused and there is no other available advocate to undertake it, it should require questions to be reduced to writing. It will assist the process, in most cases, if 'Grounds of Cross-Examination' are identified under specific headings;

- A Judge should never feel constrained to put every question the lay party seeks to ask. In this exercise the Judge will simply have to evaluate relevance and proportionality;

- Cross-examination is inherently dynamic. For it to have forensic rigour the Judge will inevitably have to craft and hone questions that respond to the answers given. The process can never become formulaic;

- It must always be borne in mind that in the overarching framework of Children Act proceedings, the central philosophy is investigative. Even though fact finding hearings, of the nature contemplated here, have a highly adversarial complexion to them the same principle applies. Thus, it may be perfectly possible, without compromising fairness to either side, for the Judge to conduct the questioning in an open and less adversarial style than that deployed in a conventional cross-examination undertaken by a party's advocate.'

Sir Andrew McFarlane concludes his judgement by offering the following practical points for courts to consider when appointment a QLR or when preparing to put questions itself:

- Whilst there is value in the QLR attending court for the ground rules hearing so that they may meet the party on whose behalf they will be asking questions, where this is impractical, and where holding the hearing remotely means that a QLR who could not otherwise act can be appointed, it should be acceptable for the QLR to attend the ground rules hearing remotely;

- The default position for the full hearing should be for the QLR to be in attendance at court, rather than joining remotely, as the overall effectiveness and fairness of the process is likely to be diminished if they are not in the courtroom;

- In all cases (whether there is a QLR or not) at the ground rules hearing, or earlier, the court should direct that the prohibited party should submit a clear statement shortly stating the allegations, facts or findings that they seek to establish;

- In all cases, the prohibited party should be required to file a written list of the questions that they wish to have asked prior to the main hearing. The list should go to the QLR, or to the court if there is no QLR, but not to the witness or other parties. This process should not prevent the prohibited party from identifying additional questions that may arise during the hearing.

Statutory Guidance

https://assets.publishing.service.gov.uk/media/665ef0d98f90ef31c23ebdb0/Qualified_legal_representative_appointed_by_the_Court_Statutory_guidance.pdf

CHAPTER TWENTY-ONE

EXPERTS

The more common experts in Family Proceedings are:

- Paediatrician (Child injury)
- Radiologist (Fractures)
- Psychiatrist (Capacity, Alcohol, drugs)
- Psychologist (Capacity, Risk assessment)
- Scientists (DNA paternity)
- Accountants (Business)
- Valuers (House and property)
- Actuaries (Pensions)

The definition of an 'expert' is 'a person who is very knowledgeable about or skillful in a particular area'. This expertise means that others can have confidence that their opinion is informed and reliable. Expert witnesses are different from other witnesses who give written or spoken evidence to a court. If someone is an expert, the court is prepared to accept their opinions about a case, rather than just evidence about what a witness has seen or heard.

The duty of an expert witness is to provide independent assistance to the court through their objective, unbiased opinion about matters within their expertise. This duty is owed to the court and overrides any duty to anyone who is instructing or paying the expert.

It is the Judge's role in cases involving children, to decide what the facts are if people can't agree, and having decided the facts, to make decisions about what is in the best interests of the child. In straightforward cases, the Judge can rely on the evidence of the witness directly involved about what did or didn't happen and will not need the assistance of an expert. However, some cases are more complicated and expert evidence is necessary so that the right decision can be made for the child. For example, if a child is physically injured and no one can say how it happened or if the court needs to know more about the mental health issues facing the parents. These are areas which can only be properly understood by people who have specialised training and experience. Social workers and Children's Guardians are considered 'experts' by the court in their own area of expertise. Experts can play a role in many different types of family cases but are more common in children and financial applications.

The 'Necessary' Test

A party must have the court's permission to instruct an expert, and this permission is only given if the party requesting the report shows that the expert report is 'necessary 'to resolve proceedings justly. Section 13(6) Children and Families Act 2014.

This test of 'necessary 'sets a hurdle which is significantly higher than the old test of what is 'reasonably required 'Re TG [2013] EWCA Civ 5 and Re HL [2013] EWCA Civ 655.

The Judgment of Lord Justice Munby in Re HL [2013] described 'necessary 'evidence as being 'indispensable 'as opposed just 'useful, reasonable and desirable'.

Under Section 13(7) Children and Families Act 2014 the court must consider:

- any impact which giving permission would be likely to have on the welfare of the children concerned
- the issues the expert evidence would relate to
- the questions which the court would require the expert to answer
- what other expert evidence is available
- whether evidence could be given by another person on the matters on which the expert would give evidence
- the impact which giving permission would be likely to have on the case and the timetable
- the cost, and
- any matters set out in the Family Procedure Rules 2010.

The Application Itself

Part 25 of the Family Procedure Rules 2010 sets out the procedure that must be followed if a party seeks permission to instruct an expert.

As a general rule, an application should be made as soon as possible.

Rule 25.6 sets out when an application is to be made and Rule 25.7 describes how it is to be made – i.e. in what form and with what supporting documents and information.

Form C2 is currently the appropriate application form to be used. There is a need to set out the field in which the expert evidence is required, identify the expert by name (if possible) so that the other parties can comment on the suitability of that particular expert. Included in the application should be a draft of the order being sought and a copy of the expert's CV, details of how long the expert will need to write a report and how much it will cost. A draft letter of instructions should be included in the papers.

The expert must have knowledge appropriate to the court case, have been active in the area of work or practice, have sufficient experience of the issues relevant to the case, be regulated or accredited to a registered body where this is appropriate, have relevant qualifications and have received appropriate training to comply with safeguarding requirements.

The Letter of Instructions

- The requirements for the letter of instruction are strict and set out in Practice Direction 25C. The letter of instruction should have already been drafted and attached to the application for the court's permission to instruct an expert. This should have been seen and agreed by all the parties to the case

- The expert is usually instructed by all the parties but one party will' take the lead'. This party will be responsible for sending the letter of instruction, ensure that the expert is available to come to court and for being the first point of contact in the case of any queries. The court must approve the questions asked which must be within the ambit of the expert's area of expertise. The expert must have a list of documents, indexed and paginated. The letter of instruction must be clear as to the basis on which the expert is being instructed to provide a report and who pays the expert's fees. If the parties are paying using their own money, it is for them to enter into a contract with the expert to pay what is agreed. If the expert is to be paid by Legal Aid, care should be taken to ensure the fees are in accordance with the Legal Aid regulations.

CHAPTER TWENTY-TWO

CAFCASS AND LOCAL AUTHORITY REPORTS

Safeguarding Letter

This is a letter that a Cafcass worker will write and send to the Family Court in a Private Children application. On receipt of a court application, Cafcass will speak to the parties (usually the parents) and ask about the child's safety and any worries that they might have. Safeguarding checks are also undertaken with the Police and the Local Authority to find out whether there are any known relevant criminal convictions, safety or welfare risks to the child. The results of these enquiries are included in the Safeguarding Letter as well as some guidance to the court as to how to progress the case. A Cafcass Officer attends the FHDRA and can speak to parties to clarify any issues and wherever possible, conduct an early dispute resolution to see whether agreement can be reached or the issues narrowed.

A Parenting Plan is often used as a framework and parents are encouraged to use the plan to focus on the needs of the child. Some cases can be resolved at first hearing by consent or with further support from local programmes, such as supported or supervised Contact Centres. The Plan can help clarify the arrangements parties need to put in place to care for the children after separation.

Section 7 Reports

A Section 7 Children Act 1989 report is a report written by a Cafcass worker or a social worker from the Local Authority in cases where an application has been made to the court under Section 8 of The Children

Act 1989. The Local Authority will prepare the report where they have had a recent involvement with the family in question.

A Section 7 report may be required in private proceedings where an application has been made to the court for an order under Section 8 Children Act 1989, which may be:

- Child Arrangements Order – specifies whom the child is to live with and/or with whom the child is to have contact;
- Prohibited Steps Order – prevents either parent from doing certain things or making specific trips with their children without the express permission of the other parent;
- Specific Issue Order – an order to determine a specific question which has or may arise in connection with any aspect in relation to a child;
- Family Assistance Order – a short-term order requiring a Cafcass officer or a social worker to advise, assist, and befriend any person in the named order.

A Section 7 report is only ordered by the court when it needs information about a child's welfare, what is best for the child and sometimes where there are certain risk factors or concerns raised in relation to a child, parent or other relative.

A Cafcass worker or social worker will provide an independent assessment of a situation and will report these findings to the court. The author of the report may be required to attend court in support of the report but only if the court directs such attendance.

The court usually stipulates what it requires Cafcass or the social worker to focus on in their report.

Contents of Section 7 Report

A Section 7 report should contain all background information, key facts and evidence stipulated in accordance with the Welfare Checklist. The report will set out the child's wishes and feelings and what the Cafcass officer or Local Authority social worker considers to be in the best interest of the child.

The worker who prepares the report may speak to the child (depending on their age and understanding) about his/her wishes and feelings and what he/she would like to happen.

They will also spend time with both parties and listen to any concerns they may have. They may also speak to others such as family members, teachers and health workers. They will not ask the child to make a decision or to choose between either parent regarding with whom they will live or the contact they will have with the non-resident parent.

Decision and Court Order

After reading the report and listening to what the parties and other people in the case have said, the court will make the final decision on the court application. This decision will be based on what is best for the child. It will take into account the wishes and feelings of the child only if this is considered to be in their best interests. The decision will be set out in a court order with which the parties must comply.

Separated Parent Information Programme

Courts have the power, by making a court order, to direct parents to attend a programme aimed at promoting safe contact with children. Cafcass is usually asked to advise the court if it is suitable for the parties to attend. There is no charge for a Cafcass service user to attend. They will not attend the same session as their ex-partner.

Rule 16.4 Appointments

Rule 16.4 of the Family Procedure Rules 2010 and Practice Direction 16A allows a child to be made a party in family proceedings and obtain legal representation in their own right. The decision to make the child a party will always be exclusively that of the court, made in the light of the facts and circumstances of the particular case. That decision will not normally be taken by the court without first taking account of the views of Cafcass. Before making the child a party, consideration should be given to whether an alternative route might be preferable, such as asking Cafcass to carry out further work or by making a referral to Social Services or by obtaining expert evidence.

The court may consider making a child party to proceedings if it is satisfied that the case meets one or more of the following criteria:

- where a Family Court Advisor has recommended the child should be made a party
- the dispute between the adult parties is such that the interests of the child are not being met
- where there is an intractable dispute or where there is implacable hostility to contact or where the child may be suffering harm associated with the contact dispute
- where the views and wishes of the child cannot be adequately met by a Section 7 Report to the court
- where an older child is opposing a proposed course of action
- where there are complex issues that necessitate separate representation of the child

- where there are international elements to the case which may necessitate discussions with overseas authorities or a foreign court

- where there are serious allegations of abuse to the child and/or allegations of domestic violence

- where the proceedings concern more than one child and the welfare of the children is in conflict or one child is in a particularly disadvantaged position

- where there is a contested issue about scientific testing.

The Children's Guardian appointed to represent the child will:

- Instruct a solicitor who specialises in Family Law and is on the Law Society Children's Panel to act for the child

- Meet with the child and the parties in the proceedings

- If age appropriate, obtain the child's wishes and feelings

- Advise the court about any work, including extra services such as expert opinions, that they believe are necessary to assist the court

- If directed by the court, write a report for the court and attend appropriate court hearings

- Provide expert advice to the court and make recommendations as to what is considered to be in the child's best interests.

CHAPTER TWENTY-THREE

COURT BUNDLES

The Court Bundle is a folder of court documents provided to the court before a hearing and should contain all the evidence the court may need for that hearing.

The Bundle may be different for each hearing. When updating the old Bundle, the same page numbers for the documents already in that Bundle should be retained.

In family cases, the court expects a Bundle to be prepared for every hearing in the Family Court or in the High Court. Courts sometimes have their local practice which needs to be followed.

Normally the solicitor for the applicant prepares the Bundle. If the applicant is a Litigant in Person the solicitor for the first named respondent will prepare the court Bundle.

If there are cross-applications, the solicitor for the party who has made their application first prepares the Bundle.

If no one in the case has a solicitor, the court will usually prepare a Court Bundle.

Documents to go into the Bundle

The Bundle will have the documents that the court needs for each hearing. In preparing a Bundle for a short directions hearing, the court is unlikely to need supporting evidence such as Police records for that hearing.

The court needs one Bundle for the hearing that includes all of the documents from the parties in the case and any other papers prepared by others, for example by Cafcass.

Documents that have not filed and served should not be included in the Court Bundle.

Bundles are always broken up into sections which are divided by file dividers alphabetically and specifically:

A. Preliminary documents

B. Applications and Orders

C. Statements and Affidavits

D. Care Plans (where appropriate)

E. Experts and other reports

F. Other documents

Preliminary documents (Section A)

Preliminary documents are not evidence, they are meant to summarise information for the Judge so that the court can understand what the case is about and the purpose of the hearing.

The preliminary documents are:

• A Case Summary

A summary of the background to the hearing limited to the issues that are relevant to the hearing. This document should be neutral between the parties.

• A Statement of Issues

This document should set out the questions the court will be asked to decide at that hearing and at the final hearing.

• A Position Statement

This document is individual for each party. It should explain to the court what a party's position is for that hearing.

• A Chronology for a final hearing.

This is a list of dates, starting with the oldest, when important things happened, for example, the dates of birth of any children, dates of incidents of domestic violence, dates of applications to court and hearings.

• A Skeleton Argument

This is a document summarising the legal points a party wishes to make and how they relate to his/her case.

• A list of essential reading for the hearing.

This is a list of the documents the Judge should read before that hearing.

• Time estimate for the hearing.

This is used at fact finding or final hearings when the Judge will hear from witnesses. Each witness should be listed with a time estimate for roughly how long it will take the court to hear from them.

Size of the Bundle

Court Bundles should not be any larger than 350 pages.

If the Bundle is larger than this, the party preparing the Bundle should raise this with the court and seek a direction to have permission for the Bundle to be larger than 350 pages.

If the Bundle is larger than 350 pages, it should be separated into 2 or more lever arch files and label each file A, B, C, ... etc.

Only one Bundle needs to be prepared for each hearing. This Bundle should be an agreed Bundle. This means it will include all of the documents that the parties want the court to see for that hearing.

The party who prepares the Bundle (usually the applicant) will put together the documents and prepare a draft index. The other party in the case should be sent the index and asked if they are happy with it. If changes need to be made or documents added or removed, then this can be done before the index is finally agreed. Once there is an agreed index, the pages can be numbered.

The Case Summary should be neutral.

Resume

- Practice Direction 27A is the authority for preparing Court Bundles in Family cases; L (Procedure: Bundles: Translation) [2015] EWFC 15; Re X Re and Y (Bundles) [2008] 2 FLR 2053

- Bundles are prepared for most hearings

- Bundles are prepared by the applicant in the proceedings unless he/she is a Litigant in Person then the Bundle is prepared by First Respondent

- Bundles should be a maximum 350 pages

- Formatted and divided in accordance with PD27A

- Filed at court and served on other parties as per court direction.

- A Witness Bundle should be prepared for a contested hearing.

CHAPTER TWENTY-FOUR

LITIGANTS IN PERSON AND MCKENZIE FRIENDS

A Litigant in Person is an individual, company or organisation who is involved in court proceedings without legal representation by a solicitor or barrister.

However, this definition does not take into account changes to legislation concerning access to legal services. For example, a Litigant in Person can be represented in court by a barrister whilst still being a Litigant in Person under the direct access system.

Some Litigants in Person have a working knowledge of court procedure and require little additional assistance in representing themselves, but other Litigants in Person have no court experience and may need some assistance.

A McKenzie Friend is someone who accompanies a Litigant in Person at a court hearing for the purpose of assisting him in such matters as taking notes, helping to organise the documents, and quietly making suggestions for example, about questions to put to a witness. Although usually a non-lawyer, the McKenzie Friend should not be thought of as a Lay Advocate and has no automatic right to address the court directly.

A McKenzie Friend can ask the court to grant him or her a right of audience which will allow him or her to appear before the Judge, address the court and call and examine witnesses. Ameyaw v McGoldrick & Others [2020] EWHC 1787 (QB)

There are strict rules in place which regulate the exercise of the right of audience. It is a criminal offence for a person to exercise a right of audience or a right to conduct litigation without the appropriate permissions. The court can limit the involvement of a McKenzie Friend if, for example, the McKenzie friend is only serving his own interests, or acts in a manner unreasonable or disruptive to the court or where a McKenzie friend effectively controls the litigation. LFA v LSL [2017] EWFC B62.

Some professional McKenzie Friends charge a fee for their services.

Duties of an advocate when dealing with Litigants in Person

A lawyer owes a duty to his/her client and also to the court and the administration of justice. Lawyers must not take unfair advantage of Litigants in Person. Behaviour which might constitute the taking of unfair advantage includes bullying, the making of unjustifiable threats, misleading behaviour, claiming a sum which cannot properly be claimed or demanding something which cannot properly be demanded. Using the law and legal procedure effectively against a Litigant in Person because the lawyer has the knowledge/skills to do so is not, however, taking unfair advantage. There is also no obligation on the part of the lawyer to assist a Litigant in Person to run their case or to take action on their behalf.

Explain but don't advise.

Explain to the Litigant in Person what he/she needs to do next. Refer them to the court rules where necessary and try to ensure they understand the next steps. Explain what they are obliged to do to comply with the court orders. For example, a lawyer might tell a Litigant in Person that they need to file and serve a witness statement but not what he/she needs to be put into the statement as this would be assisting the Litigant in Person to run their case.

Communicate Effectively

When communicating with a Litigant in Person, the lawyer should be professional, co-operative and courteous. The lawyer could send him/her a copy of the Law Society's Litigants in person: guidelines for lawyers June 2015 which contains a note formulated to assist a Litigant in Person.

The lawyer should avoid legal jargon where possible and ensure language is clear. The lawyer should encourage the Litigant in Person to seek independent legal advice at the outset of the proceedings and at appropriate stages of the case. During the preparation period the lawyer should try to return telephone calls and reply to letters promptly but is under no obligation to respond to a Litigant in Person immediately.

Preparation assistance

A Litigant in Person may not take the usual steps in the court process which a represented party would. The lawyer should expect to be responsible for court bundles and take conduct of drafting and submitting court orders. The lawyer should take a full note of any conversations he/she has with the Litigant in Person so there is a record of what was discussed and when.

Useful Guidance

Particular help in working with Litigants in Person can be found in the following publications:-

- Litigants in Person: Guidelines for Lawyers June 2015
- Good Practice Guide to Working with Litigants in Person-Resolution Family First
- Practice Guidance: McKenzie Friends (Civil and Family Courts), 12 July 2010

- A Practical Guide to Working with Litigants in Person and McKenzie Friends in Family Cases by Stuart Barlow (Law Brief Publishing March 2020)

Helpful Cases

No special treatment by the court

Tinkler v Elliott (2012) EWCA Civ 1289

The self-representing Mr Elliott failed to attend a hearing but instead submitted a medical certificate of unfitness to attend court. The High Court set aside the judgement holding that Mr Elliott had a good reason for not attending the original hearing. The Court of Appeal restored the original court's decision holding that the court rules need to be rigorously applied and that there were no special rules for a Litigant in Person.

Jones v Longley & Others (2015) EWHC 3362 (Ch)

The Court said that a Litigant in Person is not subject to any special rules and is as liable as represented litigants to have costs orders made against them.

Hobson v West London Engineering Solicitors (2013) EWHC 4425 QA

High Court decision to strike out a claim as a result of the failure by the claimant, a Litigant in Person, to comply with the rules and court orders, where the claimants inaction had serious implications for the litigation process and the defendant.

Barton v Wright Hassall LLP (2018) UKSC Civ 12

The Supreme Court decided that the civil procedure rules would not be applied differently to unrepresented litigants. While the court could offer leeway in how litigants were handled during case management hearings or during the trial, this would not usually justify applying a lower standard of compliance with rules or orders of the court The Court also indicated that solicitors should not be expected to flag up procedural mistakes made by Litigant in Person on the other side.

H (A Child) [2014] EWCA Civ 271

A maternal Grandmother appealed within private law proceedings against an order that there be no direct contact with her grandchild who lived with the mother. Ryder LJ suggested that when there is a Litigant in Person involved, they should be sworn in or affirm before they make submissions, so that there is formal evidence on the court record. The Judge should also explain to a Litigant in Person that he can ask questions through the Judge who will decide whether the questions are appropriate.

Q v Q Re B (A Child), Re C (A Child) [2014] EWFC 31

Private Law proceedings adjourned by the President as a result of the father having no access to public funds for legal representation. The President considered that as the risk assessment in part relied upon the mother's account, cross examination as to whether the recommendations remained in the event that the mother's account was incorrect, was proper and appropriate.

In accordance with FPR 2010 1.1 the court was required to act justly and ensure so far as is practicable that each case was dealt with fairly and that parties were on equal footing. To dismiss this case in such circumstances was not dealing with the matter justly and fairly. The President considered that there had to be an investigation as to whether funds could be made available for this father, it being in his interest, the child's interest and also in the wider public interest of other litigants in a similar situation. There was a risk that if the process was not fair to one parent, that unfairness may disadvantage the child.

Iqbal v Iqbal [2017] EWCA Civ 19

This was a case with a lengthy history, and where a fundamental issue was the extent to which H was able to access the wealth of his family in Pakistan. After H disengaged midway through proceedings in 2011 and returned to Pakistan, there were a number of hearings and judgments summons held in his absence. W continued to play an active role, though at times representing herself. H had been excused attendance at an interim hearing, but he had attended at the first appeal, and had filed a number of documents with the court in purported compliance with its directions. The Court of Appeal concluded that elementary procedural protections that H had a right to expect would be observed were not. The consequence was that the final hearing was procedurally unfair and the order made at the end of it must be set aside and the matter remitted for final hearing before a new Judge. The subsequent enforcement hearings including H's committal to prison for 6 weeks were wholly irregular in that no procedural protections were provided at all.

In the case of Agarwala v Agarwala [2016] EWCA Civ. 1252 at paragraph [72] Lady Justice King stated: "Whilst every Judge is sympathetic to the challenges faced by litigants in person, justice simply cannot be done through a torrent of informal, unfocussed emails, often sent directly to the Judge and not to the other parties. Neither the Judge nor the court staff can, or should, be expected to field communications of this type. In my view judges must be entitled, as part of their general case management powers, to put in place, where they feel it to be appropriate, strict directions regulating communications with the court and litigants should understand that failure to comply with such directions will mean that communications that they choose to send, notwithstanding those directions, will be neither responded to nor acted upon."

Timely Service

Re B (Litigants in Person: Timely Service of Documents) (2017) EWHC 2365 (Fam)

The Court reminded legal practitioners of the need to adapt normal practices when dealing with a Litigant in Person. Minimum service requirements should be adapted in individual cases to protect the rights of a Litigant in Person and may be necessary to prevent the intrinsic unfairness to a Litigant in Person that may arise from late service. This judgment, published with the approval of the President of the Family Division, arose from a final hearing in a child abduction case in which legal documents comprising counsel's position statement (14 pages) and four law reports (100 pages) were given at the door of the court to a non-English-speaking litigant in person. Whilst Mr Justice Peter Jackson acknowledges that the position statement was of real assistance to the court, time was wasted before the hearing whilst the mother studied the documents with the help of the court-appointed interpreter.

Mr Justice Peter Jackson reminded advocates of the obligations imposed by Practice Direction 27A concerning court bundles and, in particular, paragraph 6. He noted that paragraph 6 sets out the minimum service requirements and that they should be adapted in individual cases to protect the rights of a Litigant in Person in order to prevent the intrinsic unfairness to a Litigant in Person that may arise from late service.

McKenzie Friends

In Ameyaw v McGoldrick & Ors [2020] EWHC 1741 (QB) the Judge refused a McKenzie Friend permission to speak on behalf of a litigant, stressing the Claimant was well-educated and clearly able to speak on her own behalf.

LFA v LSL (2017) EWFC B62

In a Family Law case the husband applied for his McKenzie Friend to be granted rights of audience. This was opposed by the wife arguing that the Guidance on McKenzie Friends advised that the Court should be slow to grant any application from a Litigant in Person for a right of audience or a right to conduct litigation to a lay person, including a McKenzie Friend. The Court refused the husbands application but allowed the McKenzie Friend to remain in court to provide quiet advice to the husband. The McKenzie Friend became increasingly disruptive during the hearing. The Judge took the unusual step of excluding the McKenzie Friend from the court room for the remainder of the hearing.

CHAPTER TWENTY-FIVE

POSITION STATEMENTS AND SKELETON ARGUMENTS

Position Statements

Position Statements are common in many courts. This document is individual for each party. It should explain to the court what a party's position is for that hearing. It should be a short statement, usually one or two sides of A4 paper. Position statements can be a helpful way of getting a party's points across to the Judge and the other party clearly and concisely. The Position Statement should not contain evidence.

What to include in a Position Statement

Set out the case heading at the top of the position statement including the date and time of the court hearing. This will ensure that the court staff and the Judge know which court room and which case the position statement relates to.

General Inclusions:

- details of the parties and their relationship to one another
- what has caused the application to be made, whether negotiations have been attempted and any urgency
- if there has been any domestic abuse and whether the parties are able to safely communicate with each other including the confidentiality of any address

- what has happened since the last hearing for example, documents that have been sent to the court, documents received from the other party, any documents the parties should have sent to each other but have not been received
- compliance with any court directions with a short explanation
- any court directions that the other party has failed to comply with
- the directions your client wants the court to make at the hearing
- what outcome your client is seeking

If the case relates to Children

- your client's relationship to the children. The other party's relationship to the children
- whether the other party is having contact with the children and how this is progressing. Provide a short and concise summary of any concerns
- the outcome your client is seeking. For example, the child should live with your client and see the other parent every other weekend, or for there to be no contact between the child and the other parent
- whether the children have any special needs
- if your client seeks permission to file any further evidence with details.

If the case is for a Domestic Abuse Injunction:

- whether the other party has been served with the relevant documents. Whether he/she has tried to contact your client or breached the order in any way

- give details of orders your client needs the court to make to keep him/her safe

- details of any particular directions required at the hearing. For example, permission to file police records or a letter from a GP.

If the case relates to a Financial application:

- details of your client's current financial position

- the outcome your client is seeking

- whether your client has filed all of his/her financial documents, details of any financial disclosure outstanding and when these can be obtained.

- whether the other party has provided financial disclosure and details of documents outstanding

- what directions your client is seeking the court to make at the next hearing. Whether, for example, your client wants to instruct an expert to value a property or for the other party to provide some bank statements or company accounts.

Filing the Position Statement with the court and serving the other party

If a Position Statement is prepared, this should be sent to the court and the other party well in advance of the hearing. Most courts have email addresses for family cases which can be found on the court's website. Extra copies should be taken to court for the Judge, the other party and Cafcass just in case their copy fails to arrive in time. If the court directs your client to prepare a Position Statement for a hearing this must be filed with the court and sent to the other party by the date specified on the court order.

Skeleton Arguments

This is a document that summarises the points your client wishes to make and how they relate to his/her case. It is a chance to argue their case on paper in advance of the hearing. A Judge will often read this document before coming into court and in advance of hearing any submissions. It gives the Judge a brief synopsis of the relevant matters for the court to consider and also outlines both the agreed and disagreed issues between the parties. It is not a substitute for oral argument. The fuller detail of the arguments is heard before the court orally during the trial or hearing. There is no strict formula for a good skeleton argument but it would normally include the following:

- a heading that identifies which party filing the skeleton argument
- an introduction that states your clients' position
- a list of identified issues
- the essential facts
- the text of any key statute and/or the strongest relevant case law
- your clients' submissions
- a conclusion that states what your client is asking for

The Skeleton Argument should be as concise and focused.

Skeleton Arguments are usually required before High Court and Circuit Judges. It is unlikely that a skeleton argument is required before District

Judges or Lay Magistrates. Skeleton arguments are usually prepared for interim applications, contested hearings, final hearings and appeals.

CHAPTER TWENTY-SIX

EVIDENCE ON OATH

A witness will be shown to the witness box by the court usher. The witness should stand up to take the oath, but if he/she finds standing difficult, they can ask the Lay Magistrate or the Judge if you can sit down. They will be asked to take the oath. Sworn testimony is evidence given by a witness who has made a commitment to tell the truth. If the witness is later found to have lied whilst bound by the commitment, they can be charged with the crime of perjury.

The types of commitment can include oaths, affirmations and promises.

The commitment can come in different forms depending on the situation of the witness.

These are:

- Oath: A commitment made to the witness's deity, or on their holy book
- Affirmation: A secular variant of the oath where the witness does not have to mention a deity or holy book
- Promise: A commitment made by a witness under the age of 17, or of all witnesses if none of the accused are over the age of 17.

In England and Wales the wording is:

> Oath:
>
> I swear by [substitute Almighty God/Name of God (such as Jehovah) or the name of the holy scripture] the evidence I shall give shall be the truth, the whole truth, and nothing but the truth.
>
> Affirmation:
>
> I do solemnly and sincerely and truly declare and affirm that the evidence I shall give shall be the truth, the whole truth, and nothing but the truth.
>
> Promise:
>
> I promise before Almighty God that the evidence which I shall give shall be the truth, the whole truth, and nothing but the truth.

In the UK, a person may give testimony at any age, but will not be sworn in unless 14 years old or over.

CHAPTER TWENTY-SEVEN

DRAFTING COURT ORDERS

Generally

A draft order is simply the wording of the order that the parties in the proceedings have agreed and are asking the court to make. In many cases today, family lawyers are expected to take their laptops to court and draft orders on the day. This applies to cases where at least one party is represented. Court orders are approved by the Judge, drawn up and handed to the parties on the day of the hearing. After the Judge approves the order, it will be printed out and handed to the parties on the same day as the hearing or emailed out soon afterwards. The Judge or Legal Adviser will draft the order on the day of the hearing for cases where both parties are Litigants in Person. It is usually the lawyer for the applicant that takes the lead in producing a first draft. In cases where one party is not represented, the court expects the lawyer for the represented party to produce a draft order.

Standard or Template Orders

> 'Inordinate amounts of time and money are spent – wasted – in the process of drafting orders that could, and therefore should, be standardised. The use of standard orders produced at the press of a button will obviate the need for drafts from counsel and solicitors scribbled out in the corridor. It should assist greatly in reducing the time Judges and court staff spend approving and completing orders. And the existence of a body of standardised and judicially approved forms of order will go a long way to assisting Judges and others – mediators for example – faced with the

> increasing number of litigants in person who cannot be expected to draft their own orders' – Lord Justice Mumby

This recommendation has led to the production of a series of standardised draft court orders covering most areas of Family Proceedings.

The orders have been prepared by a working group on the basis that they must be as concise as possible and easy to understand by the parties who are increasingly self-represented.

The new orders are less prescriptive as to recitals, leaving it to Judges in any particular case to decide what they choose to include or leave out. These orders do not have the strict status of forms within Part 5 of the FPR 2010 and their use, and although very strongly encouraged, are not mandatory.

A Standard Order may be varied by the court or a party if a variation is required by the circumstances of a particular case. There will be many circumstances when a variation is required and departure from the standard form will not prevent an order being valid and binding. It is expected that as many Judges and Justices' Legal Advisers as possible will use the Judicial Template to produce the new orders.

To be enforceable, penal and warning notices must be prominently displayed on the front of the order.

The orders are separated into:

- Allocation and Gatekeeping
- Case Management Directions and Section 8 and other orders
- Enforcement.

Practitioners have access to the same orders as Judges so that they can draft consistently.

Child Arrangements Programme (CAP) Master Copy Orders are available in most courts, as well as the Internet.

Recitals in Family Court Orders

The purpose of a recital in an order is, amongst other things, to record the parties' non-binding expression of intent.

Recitals are often used to cover issues that the court could not otherwise order. For example "neither party should criticise the other".

A recital is different to a direction being recorded in the body of the order. When recorded in the body of the order the direction forms part of the order and as such, is enforceable by the court.

When agreeing an order, it is important to recognise when appropriate to record an agreement in a recital or the body of the order as this can have important consequences for the parties.

President's Guidance: Forms of Orders in Children Cases was issued by Sir Andrew McFarlane, President of the Family Division, on 17 June 2019.

The guidance stated that recitals in the first order and last order in any child case (public or private law) should be treated differently to recitals in any interim orders – Paragraph 9:

> "the first order made in any child case (public or private law) should comply with the previous Practice Guidance or PD12B, para 14.13, so that the key information in each case is recorded there. For subsequent orders (other than final orders) the court, while following the previous Practice Guidance, should tailor the order to the particular circumstances of the case, without the need to include

> lengthy narrative material which does not relate to the requirements of the particular order. The minimum required content in an order following a second or subsequent interim hearing will be:
>
> - a recital of who attended and their representation;
> - a recital of the issues determined at the hearing;
> - a record of any agreement or concession made during the hearing;
> - a recital of the issues that remain outstanding; and
> - the text of any orders that were made.
>
> It is expected that this approach will enable the court to limit the content of orders to what is strictly required for effective case management.
>
> Following a final hearing, the court order should, as has always been the case, set out in full the orders that the court has made, together with any appropriate recitals".

https://www.judiciary.uk/publications/president-of-the-family-divisions-guidance-forms-of-orders-in-children-cases/

As stated above, the first order should comply with PD12B para 14.13 as follows:

> "Order (other than a final order) – Where no final agreement is reached, and the court is required to give case management directions, the following shall be included on the order:
>
> - the date, time and venue of the next hearing;

- whether the author of any section 7 report is required to attend the hearing, in order to give oral evidence. A direction for the Cafcass officer or WFPO to attend court will not be made without first considering the reason why attendance is necessary, and upon what issues the Cafcass officer or WFPO will be providing evidence"

Consent Orders

Care should be taken in the drafting of Consent Orders. Take note of the following:

- the court has no additional powers simply because there is an agreement. Recitals may be needed as an alternative
- the difference between recitals and orders
- the difference between recitals and undertakings
- the meaning of an undertaking and how can it be enforced.

In Financial cases:

- there can be no orders against third parties.
- orders can only be made under sections 22 to 24 MCA
- the court has jurisdiction, for example, after decree nisi for final orders
- state the position on costs.

In Private Children cases:

Parents commonly reach an agreement regarding contact and residence. but these informal agreements are not automatically legally binding and have limited means of recourse if the opposing parent acts in breach of that informal agreement.

Consent Orders provide a mechanism to make an informal agreement legally binding and therefore enforceable through the Family Court. This informal agreement can be incorporated into a court order. It will need to be signed and dated and attached to a C100 court form.

There is no legal requirement to attend Mediation (MIAM) prior to applying to court for a Consent Order. The court will ensure that the agreement reached is in the best interests of the children concerned.

There will generally be a hearing to which both parties will be invited to attend where the court will verify that the agreement has been reached by consent. Safeguarding checks need to be conducted before the court can make the agreed order.

Revised Family Court Orders

On 21 May 2024, Peel J made the following announcement via the Judiciary website:

I make this announcement with the authority of the President (of the Family Division).

On 17 May 2023 the updated Standard Orders and House Rules were released after a comprehensive review. A handful of minor amendments were made pursuant to a release on 24 October 2023.The Standard Orders group has continued to monitor the orders contained in Volume 1 (finance) and Volume 2 (children and others) in the light of developments in law and practice.

This release is intended to address developments since May 2023.The main changes are as follows:

Orders 1.1 (para 81), 1.2 (para 52), 7.0 (para 72) and 7.1 (para 7) requiring the parties to file a new Form FM5 pursuant to the Family Procedure (Amendment No 2) Rules 2023 (SI/2023/1324 of which the relevant parts came into force on 29 April 2024. Orders enabling the court to adjourn so that the parties may attend non court dispute resolution are already incorporated at 1.1 (para 73), 7.0 (para 43) and 7.1 (para 14).The correct rule (7.19(5)) as opposed to the previous reference to 7.32(5) has been included in orders 1.1 and 1.2 in respect of applying for decree absolute/final divorce order more than 12 months after decree nisi/conditional divorce order. Updates to financial orders 6.1-6.3 and children orders 22.1-22.4 in respect of arbitrations.

Inclusion in orders financial orders 1.1 and 1.2 of provision for interpreters.

Recasting of the **child arrangements order** warnings and the confidentiality warnings to better reflect the provisions of (i) s12 of the Administration of Justice Act 1960 and (ii) s11I, s13 and s97 of the Children Act 1989.

New or amended orders at 7.10, 7.11, 11.2 and 11.3 to reflect the provisions of the **Police Disclosure Protocol** dated 1 March 2024.

A new police disclosure order at 10.3.

Updates to provisions in respect of **QLRs** at 1.1 (paras 76 and 77), series 7, series 8 and 24.1-24.7.

Amendments to orders for **disclosure of the whereabouts of a child** in series 9 and series 13 so that the address of the child may only be disclosed to the court in the first instance and not to the applicant without permission of the court. This is likely to become a rule later this year and is considered to be good practice before such a rule comes into force.

A new Presumption of Death Order at 19.3.

An updated email address for orders against the Home Office under 9.6.

The revised and updated Standard Orders are attached as are, for completeness, the House Rules which are unchanged.

CHAPTER TWENTY-EIGHT

APPEALS

Parties should be advised that they should not submit an appeal just because they do not agree with the court's decision. They are required to show they have grounds to appeal the decision made by the court.

Grounds of appeal

This is a need to show that the decision of the Judge or Lay Magistrates of the lower court was:

1. wrong, or
2. unjust because of a serious procedural or other irregularity in the Proceedings in the lower court.

There is a need to show that the Judge/Lay Magistrates did not apply the law correctly, did not follow the correct procedure, or that there are other strong reasons why the decision was wrong or unfair.

Time limits

There is a strict 21-day time limit to submit an appeal for a final order.

If this time has expired, a party can ask for permission to submit the appeal out of time. This should be set out on the Application to Appeal Form with an explanation as to why the appeal was not made within the 21-day time limit. The Judge will consider the reasons for the delay and the effect of the delay on the case.

The courts dealing with an appeal

Decisions made by Lay Magistrates or a District Judge sitting in the Family court will be heard by a Circuit Judge sitting in the Family Court.

Decisions made by a District Judge of the High Court, a Circuit Judge or Recorder in Private Law Child Proceedings will be heard by a High Court Judge sitting in the High Court.

Decisions by a District Judge (Principal Registry of Family Division) in Proceedings for financial remedy will be heard by a Judge of High court Judge level sitting in the Family Court.

Decisions made by a High Court Judge sitting in the High Court, Circuit Judge or Recorder in Public Law Child Proceedings will be heard at the court of Appeal.

Permission

A party will not be required to obtain permission to submit an appeal if the decision was made by Lay Magistrates or a District Judge sitting in the Family Court. A party will be required to obtain permission if the decision was made by any other Judge. This should generally be requested orally at the hearing when the decision is made. If the Judge refuses permission to appeal, a party can seek permission to appeal from the Appeal Court. This request can be made in the appeal notice which is lodged with the Appeal Court.

Once an appeal has been submitted, the court will consider whether to grant the party permission. It can refuse permission on the basis of the application without holding a hearing. However, this will usually be where a party has exceeded the time limit to submit the appeal.

In most appeals, the parties will be informed of a date of a hearing whereby the Appeal Judge will look over the appeal papers submitted, hear any submissions and ask questions about the application. The Judge will then decide whether the appeal has a real prospect of success or whether there is any other compelling reason why you should be given permission to appeal.

How to submit an appeal

The application to appeal is by way of an Appellant's Notice. If the appellant is appealing to the High Court he/she will need to complete the FP161 form. If the appeal is to any other court, N161 form should be completed. There is a need to give reasons for the appeal, including the grounds relied on.

Costs

If an appeal fails, the appellant can be asked to pay the legal costs of the other party. This is one of the reasons why a party should be advised to be cautious about submitting an appeal.

Alternatives

If a party is unhappy with the terms of an order and wishes to change these, he/she could consider making an Application for Variation at a later stage, likewise with the discharge of the court order.

CHAPTER TWENTY-NINE

ENFORCEMENT HEARINGS

Enforcement of a Child Arrangements Order

An application for Enforcement is made on a Form C79. Enforcement proceedings must be dealt with without delay and if possible, listed before the Judge or Lay Magistrates that dealt with matters previously.

Section 11J of Children Act 1989 provides:

If the court is satisfied beyond reasonable doubt that a person has failed to comply with the provisions of the Child Arrangements Order, it may make an Enforcement Order imposing on the person an Unpaid Work requirement. The court may not make an Enforcement Order if it is satisfied that the person had a reasonable excuse for failing to comply with the order. The burden of proof lies on the person claiming to have had a reasonable excuse, and the standard of proof is the balance of probabilities. The court may make an Enforcement Order in relation to the Child Arrangements Order only on the application of a person who is, for the purposes of the Child Arrangements Order, the person with whom the child concerned lives or is to live; a person whose contact with the child concerned is provided for in the Child Arrangements Order; any individual subject to a condition under section 11(7)(b) or an activity condition imposed by the child arrangements order; or the child concerned. Where the person proposing to apply for an enforcement order in relation to a Child Arrangements Order is the child concerned, the child must obtain the leave of the court before making such an application. The court may grant leave to the child concerned only if it is satisfied that he has sufficient understanding to make the proposed application. The court may suspend an Enforcement Order for such period as it thinks fit. The court can make more than one Enforcement Order in relation to the same person on the same occasion.

Matters to consider when deciding to enforce an order

Practice Direction 12B Child Arrangements Programme Paragraph 21.1 states:

When the court receives an application to enforce a Child Arrangements Order, it will consider the following:

- whether the facts for the alleged non-compliance are agreed or whether it is necessary to conduct a hearing to establish them
- the reasons for any non-compliance
- the wishes and feelings of the child
- whether any advice is required from Cafcass on the appropriate way forward
- assess and manage any risks of making further or other Child Arrangements Orders
- whether a Separated Parents Information Programme or referral for dispute resolution is appropriate
- whether an Enforcement Order may be appropriate
- the Welfare Checklist.

Penalties for Breaching a Court Order

At the top of all Child Arrangements Order there is a warning notice that sets out the consequences to both parties as to what will happen if they do not comply with the order.

There are powers available to the court as set out in Practice Direction 12B paragraph 21.6 when considering an application to enforce.

These are:

- referral of both parents to a Separated Parents Information Programme or Mediation
- unpaid work requirement of between 40 and 200 hours where the court is satisfied beyond a reasonable doubt that one party has failed to comply with a provision of the Order (Schedule A1 Section 9(2) (a-b) & Section 9(9) Children Act 1989)
- committal to prison (in very rare/serious cases)
- changing which party the child or children live with (in very extreme/serious cases) or variation of the Child Arrangements Order to include a more defined order
- a fine
- an order for compensation for financial loss (Section 110 Children Act 1989)
- a Contact Enforcement Order or Suspended Enforcement Order (Section 11J Children Act 1989)
- a Family Assistance Order (Section 16 Children Act 1989)
- the court can vary a child arrangements order if it considers it to be in the best interests of the child to do so.

Breaching Spousal Maintenance Orders

If an ex-partner stops paying this maintenance, the courts have the power to enforce the order under part 33 of the Family Procedure Rules 2010 and could also order for the arrears to be paid immediately.

With an enforcement, the person responsible for paying the spousal maintenance can be liable to pay the arrears and the interest on the unpaid amount of spousal maintenance. Such an action must be bought within 12 months to bring an enforcement. Where the arrears are more than 12 months, permission will be needed from the court to collect these. The court could also issue a Judgement Summons which carries a threat of imprisonment where a breach takes place.

The Approach of the Court in Enforcement Proceedings

Whether the breach is of an order regarding a child or an order in respect of money, the approach is the same: the breach has to be proved beyond reasonable doubt, and the punishment that is imposed will be partly by way of punishment and partly in order to secure compliance. The longest prison sentence that can be imposed is two years. The maximum is six weeks, where the committal is for non-payment of debt under a judgment summons.

Contempt of Court in Family Proceedings

There are five main categories of contempt:

- Failure to Comply with a Court Order to do an act, or not to do something, such as failure to hand over a child, failure to comply with orders to provide documents or otherwise deliberately not to follow court orders. The maximum penalty is two years imprisonment

- Publicising information about proceedings (eg about children or about private matters from family proceedings): Penalty up to two years imprisonment

- Failure to comply with a Domestic Abuse (Non-Molestation') Order where, in addition to contempt proceedings in the family courts, prosecution is by the Police or following a power of arrest attached by the court

- Contempt in the face of the court and interference with the due administration of justice (eg, calling judges 'Enemies of the People', or discouraging your opponent from pursuing their case)

- Judgement Summons. Failure to pay sums of money where the maximum penalty is 6 weeks imprisonment. The Judgment Summons Procedure which is still available in family courts under Section 5 Debtors Act 1869. This applies where money is said not to have been paid, but it is rarely used by the courts as a means of enforcement because other newer methods are available and more effective.

CHAPTER THIRTY

COMMON TYPES OF FAMILY COURT ORDERS

Overview of Children Orders

The Children Act 1989 is the main source of law that governs relationships between children and their parents. Disputes between separated parents are called Private Law Proceedings. This is because the dispute is between the individuals, and does not actively involved Government Agencies concerned with Child Protection e.g. Social Services.

Where those Government Agencies are involved, in the form of a Local Authority's Social Services Department, this is because there is a concern about the risk to a child from some feature of Family life. The risk may be to the child's physical, emotional or mental health and may be active (e.g. through abuse) or passive (such as through neglect). Proceedings involving Social Services are called Public Law Proceedings.

Parental Responsibility

Parental Responsibility (PR) is the name for the Bundle of rights many people assume one has by being a parent, namely the right to make decisions about a child's upbringing. The Children Act 1989 defines PR as "All the rights, duties, powers, responsibilities and authority which by law a parent of a child has in relation to the child and his property".

A person who has PR is entitled to a say in all important matters including the child's upbringing. Examples of issues where a person with PR is entitled to be involved in decision making include:-

1. whether the child should undergo medical treatment;

2. where and how the child is educated;

3. what the child should be named and whether there should be any change to that;

4. how the child's property should be dealt with;

5. when and how the child should be represented in legal Proceedings;

6. the child's religious upbringing; and

7. whether the child should travel abroad, either for a holiday or to live.

It should be noted that Parental Responsibility is separate from decisions like where a child lives (residence) and whom he or she sees (contact).

Although having parental responsibility gives a parent certain rights, there is an obligation to exercise those rights for the benefit of the child. Where there is dispute as to how PR should be exercised, the court will look at what outcome best meets the child's needs, not which parental rights should be prioritised.

Mothers automatically have parental responsibility from the moment of the child's birth. A father will automatically have parental responsibility if he was married to the mother either at the time of the child's birth, or subsequently. A father who is not married to the mother will only have parental responsibility automatically if the child was born after December 2003 and he is named on the birth certificate.

In all other circumstances, a father will not automatically have PR and must obtain it by agreement with the child's mother, or by court Order. In some families, people other than the child's parents, will have parental responsibility, but almost always by way of court Order.

Child Arrangements Orders

A Child Arrangements Order confirms where a child will live and with whom, and when they will spend time with a person or people other than those they normally live with. This is usually the non-resident parent, although can include grandparents and other relatives.

The court will make a Child Arrangements Order if parents are unable to agree on the arrangements for where a child lives and when they spend time with their non-resident, for example, a Child Arrangements Order can deal with:-

1. which parent the child will live with;
2. how much time the child will spend with the other parent (if any);
3. when a child will spend time with the other parent;
4. whether Contact with the other parent should be supervised.

An arrangement called Shared Care is becoming increasingly popular. It can provide for a child to live with both parents and spell out (within the CAO) how the time will be divided. A shared Care arrangement can be made even if the division of time is unequal between the two homes.

Please note that the terminology of the Children Act 1989 has changed over the years. Old expressions such as "Custody" and "Access" are often used, even though the terms disappeared many years ago. These were succeeded by the terms "Residence" and "Contact" which are no longer in existence. Orders made under the previous rules, will of course still exist.

Prohibited Steps Orders

A Prohibited Steps Order (PSO) is an Order that forbids someone from exercising their powers of parental responsibility in a particular manner.

PSOs can cover many areas. Some of the more common examples of PSOs include forbidding a parent to:-

1. remove the child from the UK;

2. change the child's name or allow him or her to be known by another name;

3. change the child's school; and

4. take the child for identified medical treatment.

PSO's may be made against any person (not just a child's parent) so a PSO could be made against a Family member or friend who it was feared might make a decision of a type usually taken by someone with PR.

Specific Issue Orders

A Specific Issue Order (SIO) is made where a dispute arises about a question of PR. The disagreement facing the court dealing with an SIO is usually narrow and well-defined.

Examples of matters that might be the basis of an SIO include:-

1. which school a child should attend;

2. whether a child should have a particular course of treatment (such as a vaccination or operation);

3. in which religious rights the child should participate (for example circumcision; confirmation); and

4. whether the child should temporarily leave the UK for a holiday.

The court will be asked to grant permission for a particular course of action i.e. a dispute between the parents or others with PR.

Child Arrangements Orders, PSOs and SIOs are sometimes referred to as Section 8 Orders. This is because the court's power to make them comes from Section 8 of the Children Act 1989.

Most parents are entitled, as of right, to apply for a Section 8 Order relating to their children. Other Family members and significant people in a child's life might also be able to apply for a Section 8 Order as of right. Those who cannot, need to ask the court for permission to make the Application.

Section 8 Orders, once made, usually last until the child concerned reaches 16. In exceptional circumstances, an Order can last until the child reaches 18.

When considering whether to make a Section 8 Order, the court's first and overriding obligation is to the welfare of the child.

The court is required to have regard to a number of matters known as the Welfare Checklist.

The court will proceed on the basis that delay in resolving a dispute about Section 8 Orders is likely to prejudice the welfare of the child.

The court will not make a Section 8 Order unless it considers that doing so would be better for the child than making no Order at all. This is called the "No Order" principle.

Appointment or Removal of a Guardian

The Children Act 1989 introduces a concept of a child's Guardian. A Guardian is a person who assumes responsibility for, and has parental responsibility for, a child on the death of his or her parents.

A parent with PR may appoint a Guardian in writing (this is often done in a Will). The appointment only takes effect once all parents with PR for the child have died.

The court also has the power to appoint a Guardian if there is no-one with PR.

The court will take into account the same matters in deciding a question about Guardianship as it does when dealing with Section 8 Orders.

Special Guardianship Orders

A Special Guardianship Order appoints one or more people as Special Guardians of the child. The Order lasts until the child is 18 (unless it is changed by way of court Order before then). The Special Guardian has parental responsibility for the child and can take most decisions about the child (such as where the child will live or go to school) without having to consult anyone else. The Special Guardian cannot change the child's surname or take them abroad for more than three months without the agreement of anyone else with parental responsibility or the permission of the court.

A Special Guardianship Order will enable the child to keep ties with their birth Family, although the family's rights and responsibilities are reduced.

Adoption Orders

When the child is adopted, he or she becomes part of their "new" adoptive Family and all legal ties with their birth Family are cut. The natural parents lose their parental responsibility and the Adoption Order cannot, except in extremely rare occasions, be varied or discharged.

Non-Molestation Orders

A Non-Molestation Order is a type of court Injunction. It can be used to prevent a partner or ex-partner from displaying violent or threatening behaviour towards a man or woman and/or their children. This includes intimidation, pestering and harassment.

A Non-Molestation Order may stop a particular person:-

1. being on the same road as the home or child's school;
2. contacting the person concerned;
3. damaging property; and
4. communicating with you other than through a third party.

It should be noted that a breach of a Non-Molestation Order will be a criminal offence and the Police are entitled to arrest the offender and bring them before the criminal court as well as the Family court.

Occupation Orders

An Occupation Order is a type of court Injunction. It can be used to control who lives in the Family home. It can also restrict a particular person from entering the area surrounding the Family home.

Occupation Orders are often used alongside Non-Molestation Orders. They help people who want to remain in the Family home, but who are scared to do so because of the threat of domestic violence.

With an Occupation Order, a violent ex-partner can be prevented from being in the property or coming near it even if the property is rented or subject to a mortgage. Other additional provisions can be made as part of any Occupation Order e.g. the payment of the mortgage or rent.

Orders for Financial Provision for a Child

Financial support for a child will usually be by reference to the Child Maintenance Services (CMS) who will calculate a level of child support payable by an absent parent by way of a formula applicable to most parents.

There are some situations where the CMS will not be able to assist, or where the formula may be less helpful. These include the following:-

1. some families where either the parents or the child ordinarily live outside of the UK;
2. if the paying parents net income is more than £104,000 per annum;
3. where a child has special needs; and
4. where a child is beyond secondary education.

In these situations, the court retains the ability to look at what level of regular financial support is suitable. This is under Schedule 1 of the Children Act 1989. The court will be guided by, but not bound by, the CMS formulas.

Beyond the question of regular financial support, there are other types of financial provision to benefit a child that a court is able to Order under Section 1. One very common example is where there is a dispute about parents 'contributions towards school fees. Private school fees are not dealt with by the CMS and an application to court would need to be made if there were any disagreements about who ought to pay.

The court will take into account all the Family circumstances.

Under Schedule 1, the definition of a child's "parent" is wider than normal. It includes a child's biological mother and father but also any other person to whom they are or were married, so long as the child was 'treated as a child of the Family'. An application under Section 1 might be made, against a step-parent or former step-parent.

Matrimonial Financial Orders following Divorce

These are found in the Matrimonial Causes Act 1973 and include Maintenance Pending Suit, Periodical payments, Property transfer orders and Pension Orders. The court has a wide discretion as to orders it can make usually encompassed within the Act.

Cohabitation & Same Sex Relationships

The court has the power to make various orders in the event of a couple separating.

CHAPTER THIRTY-ONE

FUNDING A FAMILY LAW CASE

Introduction

a. At the outset of a case, usually during the first interview, the solicitor will discuss with the client the question of how the case is going to be paid for. The solicitor must send the client the terms of business, including costs, of the firm. This is usually in a separate letter (often referred to as client care letter) and sent in duplicate, requiring the client to sign and return one copy, which should be placed on the client's file.

b. It is the duty of the solicitor to update the client throughout the case as to the fees which have been incurred and are likely to be incurred. Interim bills can be sent out as the case progresses to cover the ongoing work of the solicitor.

c. Solicitors often require money to be paid into their client account to cover any outgoings which they may incur on their client's behalf such as the court fees for issuing a divorce petition.

Methods of funding cases

- **The Hourly Rate** is the main way in which lawyers are paid for their work in family cases. Charging rates are set by the firm and vary according to location and seniority of the Solicitor dealing with the case.

- **Deferred Payment of Legal Fees**, also called *Sears Tooth* agreements can be entered into whereby lawyers can opt to wait until a case is finalised before requiring payment. Deferred payments are likely to be available only where there is insufficient income to meet the lawyer's fees but there is sufficient capital, which once unlocked, can pay the fees.

- **Court Orders** can also be used to secure payment of lawyers' fees, which is dealt with under ss 49–54 Legal Aid, Sentencing and Punishment of Offenders Act 2012 which allows the court to order a party to make payment to their former spouse or civil partner for their legal costs, which will be known as a Legal Services Payment Order (LSPO). This type of order under s22ZA Matrimonial Causes Act 1973 is available in proceedings for divorce/dissolution/(judicial) separation and in connected financial relief proceedings.

- **Funded by loans** where there is no other way of funding a case. Specialist family litigation loans are available to fund family cases. (https://www.ifa-direct.com).

- **Other Funding Options.** Fixed fees are becoming more widespread in family cases. It used to be the situation that only initial interviews were conducted on a fixed-fee bases but now clients can secure fixed fees for each element of their case. This is becoming more common as clients are choosing to do a lot of the routine work themselves (such as preparing their own financial statements), only requiring the Solicitor to do certain elements of the case. This practice called "unbundling".

- **Legal Aid**

  Legal aid available for a limited range of family cases including:

  - domestic abuse cases under Part IV of the Family Law Act 1996

- private family cases where there is evidence of domestic abuse
- public family law proceedings regarding the protection of children
- representation for children who are made parties to private family proceedings
- wardship
- child abduction
- forced marriage protection order proceedings
- legal advice in support of mediation

For those clients eligible for legal aid, they must pass both a means and a merits test. This means their financial position will be looked at. Those in receipt of certain welfare benefits will automatically be eligible under the means test. The merits test asks if there is "sufficient benefit" to the client being allowed legal advice. This ensures that advice is not given on trivial matters. To qualify for legal aid on the basis that the applicant or their child(ren) has been the victim of domestic abuse or violence and evidence must be provided. **Civil Legal Aid (Procedure) (Amendment) (No 2) Regulations 2017, SI 2017/1237**

Statutory charge

The statutory charge is the means by which costs payable out of the legal aid fund in relation to proceedings under which money or property has been recovered or preserved are repaid to the fund. A solicitor is under a duty to protect the legal aid fund and no monies can be paid to the client in respect of any costs, lump sum or sale proceeds ordered (or agreed) to be paid to the client, or any other capital recovered or preserved by court order or agreement. Sufficient monies must be retained by the solicitor to cover the full amount of the statutory charge.

Legal Aid, Sentencing and Punishment of Offenders Act 2012, Sch 1, Pt 1

Civil Legal Aid (Procedure) Regulations 2012, SI 2012/3098, regs 4–10

Civil Legal Aid (Merits Criteria) Regulations 2013, SI 2013/104, SI 2013/104

https://www.gov.uk/government/organisations/legal-aid-agency

CHAPTER THIRTY-TWO

COSTS IN FAMILY PROCEEDINGS

Generally speaking, each party will be liable to pay their own legal costs incurred within court proceedings relating to arrangements for children, however there are circumstances where one party can be ordered to pay the costs of the other.

What is the legal basis for a costs order?

Section 51(1) of the Senior Courts Act 1981 provides that, subject to rules of court, costs shall be ordered at the discretion of the court.

In family cases, the relevant rule governing the award of costs is Rule 28.1 of the Family Procedure Rules 2010 which provides that: "The court may at any time make such order as to costs as it thinks just".

How does the Judge decide whether a costs order is justified?

In deciding what order (if any) to make about costs, the court will consider the following factors:

2. All the circumstances, including the conduct of all the parties. The conduct of the parties includes:

    - conduct before, as well as during, the proceedings and in particular the extent to which the parties followed any relevant pre-action protocol;

    - whether it was reasonable for a party to raise, pursue or contest a particular allegation or issue;

- the manner in which a party has pursued or defended their case or a particular allegation or issue;

- whether the party that succeeded in making the application, in whole or in part, exaggerated their case.

2. The overriding objective.

The overriding objective set out in the Family Procedure Rules, which includes dealing with the case in ways which are proportionate to the nature, importance and complexity of the issues and save expense.

3. Previous cases.

A Judge will also consider the following core principles that have been established in previous cases when deciding how to exercise their discretion on costs:

- There is a wide discretion in relation to the award of costs.

- Costs do not ordinarily follow the event in family proceedings, as they do in other forms of civil proceedings (i.e. in family cases if you "lose" you don't pay the other parties costs).

- Where the debate surrounds the future of a child, the aspiration is that in their outcome the child is the 'winner' and indeed the only 'winner'. The court does not wish the possibility of an order for costs to discourage those with a proper interest in the child from participating in the debate. Nor does it wish to reduce the chance of their co-operation around the future life of the child by casting one as the successful party entitled to their costs and another as the unsuccessful party obliged to pay them. It is important for the parties to be able to work together in the interests of the children both during and after the proceedings. Children's lives do not stand still, stigmatising one party as the 'loser' and adding to that the burden of having to pay the other party's costs is likely to jeopardise the chances of their co-operating in the future.

- It can generally be assumed that all parties to the case are motivated by concern for the child's welfare.

- An award of costs in family proceedings may be justified if it is demonstrated that the conduct of the party (before as well as during the proceedings and/or in the manner in which a case has been pursued or defended) has been "reprehensible or unreasonable".

- Orders for costs between the parties may diminish the funds available to meet the needs of the family, although not making an order for costs may have the same effect.

Costs in Children Act cases

- The basic position remains – costs orders in private law (and public law) cases are exceptional. Any privately paying client must be advised from the outset that they are highly unlikely to recover their costs, even if they are successful.

- The only areas with some flexibility are applications or hearings which do not directly involve a consideration of the child's welfare, but are more geared towards resolving factual or legal disputes: a) a fact-finding hearing b) a declaration as to parentage c) a declaration as to habitual residence

- In Re J [2010] 1 FLR 1893 the Court of Appeal (Ward LJ and Wilson LJ) awarded a mother two thirds of her costs after her allegations of violence were found proved. That led to a raft of costs applications in fact-finding cases. Costs (Children Act)

- However in Re T [2013] 1 FLR 133 the Supreme Court gave this reminder: "The general practice of not awarding costs against a party, including a local authority, in the absence of reprehensible behaviour or an unreasonable stance, was one that accorded with the ends of justice and which should not be subject to an exception in the case of split hearings. The judge's costs order was founded on that practice and should not have been reversed by the Court of Appeal."

- This was upheld in Re S [2015] 2 FLR 208 (another hearing about care proceedings rather than private law proceedings)

- It therefore remains to be argued in private law proceedings that failing to admit allegations which are proved, or making allegations which are found to be false, is both "reprehensible" and "unreasonable".

- Where allegations are found to have been minimised/exaggerated, or where they are found but not considered significant enough to make a difference, then recovering costs is going to be unlikely.

- The impact on the paying party of making a costs order is likely to be given weight in Children Act cases.

General provisions

The relevant costs provisions are set out FPR Part 28 and PD28A. The general principles are:

- The court may at any time make an order as to costs as it thinks is just (i.e., discretion as to costs), FPR Rule 28.1.

- The general rule that costs follow the event are disapplied in private law proceedings (the opposite to civil proceedings), FPR Rule 28.2.

- Costs orders in private law proceedings are rare.

The reasoning behind the court's approach is that a costs order will reduce the funds available to meet the needs of the child, proceedings are inquisitorial, it is likely to increase tensions between the parties, impede future co-operation and it may deter a party from bringing an application which may be in the best interests of the child.

CPR Rule 44.2(4)-(5) applies within private law proceedings at first instance and on appeal. The court shall have regard to:

- Whether a party has succeeded on whole or part of their case.

- The conduct of the parties, including:

- conduct before and during the proceedings;

- whether it was reasonable for a party to raise, pursue or contest an allegation or issue;

- the manner in which a party pursued or defended an allegation or issue; and

- whether the party who succeeded has in whole or part exaggerated their claim.

The court's approach was summarised in ***Re T (a child) (order for costs)*** **[2005] EWCA Civ 311** [36] and [50]:

- *"…costs awarded against one parent or another are exceptional since the court is anxious to avoid the situation where a parent may feel "punished" by the other parent which will reduce co-operation between them. This will only impinge ultimately on the welfare of the child or the children concerned."*

- *"The conduct of the parties is in reality the major consideration when deciding whether or not an exceptional order for costs should be made. It should only be made if the penalised party has been unreasonable in his or her conduct. Moreover the "unreasonableness" must relate to the conduct of the litigation rather than the welfare of the child."*

- *"One has to be very careful in this distinction when, as in the case of (the mother), the apparent unreasonableness is as a result of the personality of the relevant party. In such circumstances, there is often an overlap of that party's conduct of the litigation and the conduct relating to the welfare of the child."*

- *"We recognise that irrational behaviour is commonplace in complex contact disputes, and that such behaviour may well be exacerbated by the personality of the individual parent. There is, however, in our judgment, a limit to which allowance can be made for a parent who deliberately and unreasonably obstructs contact by the other parent in circumstances where, on any objective analysis, contact is in the interests of the child and should take place."*

Giving notice

When seeking costs, it is good practice to give the other side notice of your application. A costs schedule should be served not less than 24 hours prior to the hearing (usually by way of Form N260). Although serving a schedule less than 24 hours prior may not be fatal, the court may take this into account and any reasonable excuse when determining the application, CPR PD44.

Assessment of costs

The court may assess a party's costs on a standard basis (costs allowed that are proportionate to the matters in issue) or indemnity basis. Usually, costs are assessed on the standard basis. If the order is silent as to which basis the costs will be assessed on, they will be assessed on the standard basis.

The court will need to determine whether the costs are assessed during the proceedings or at the conclusion of the proceedings which can be done on a summary assessment or detailed assessment.

Summary assessment is 'there and then' and usually for hearings lasting 1-day or less. The court has a wide discretion in respect of summary assessment. A case should not be summarily assessed where the receiving party is legally aided or is a child or protected party unless the solicitor has waived the right to further costs.

Detailed assessment would not normally be undertaken until the end of the proceedings and follows a specific procedure set out in CPR PD47.

The court may 'reserve' costs until the conclusion of the proceedings. The order should clearly set out which costs are being reserved until when and should be reserved to the judge making the order.

Examples of where costs orders have been made

- A party unreasonably rejecting mediation unless the other party agreed to a shared residence order whilst ignoring Cafcass recommendations to the contrary and maintaining this position until 4 days prior to a 3-day hearing, *M v H (Costs: Residence Proceedings)* [2000] 1FLR 394.

- A father was ordered to pay 2/3 of the mother's costs of a fact-finding hearing where the majority of the mother's allegations were proven (14 out of 20, inclusive of some partial admissions), *Re J (Costs of Fact Finding Hearing)* [2009] EWCA Civ 1350.

- Where a party applied for a child arrangements order when the child was rising 16 years old and there were no exceptional circumstances.

- Where the mother attempted to bribe a police officer to bring a spurious case against the father to support her case, *Timokhina v Timokin* [2019] EWCA Civ 1284.

- Defending an appeal and re-hearing of an application to re-locate out of the jurisdiction, *Costs: Leave to Remove – Re S (Leave to Remove: Costs)*[2009] EWHC 3120 (Fam).

- The father unreasonably persisted with his application for residence on the grounds that the mother was a risk to the child after two psychiatrists advised to the contrary, father being ordered to pay 80% of the mother's costs from the date that the psychiatrists filed their joint accord, *Re B (Costs)* [1999] 2 FLR 221.

- The father made a number of groundless allegations of serious conduct against the mother which had been fabricated by him, *Re G (Contact Proceedings: Costs)* [2013] EWCA Civ 1017.

Litigants in person

A litigant in person may be entitled to a costs order. However, the costs order will be limited to:

- work and disbursements that would have been allowed, if they had been undertaken by a legal representative on their behalf;
- any reasonable costs incurred for legal services, or the costs of an expert in costs in assessing the costs claim;
- provable financial loss relating to time lost that was reasonably spent on the case, or; and
- if no financial loss can be proved, then £19 per hour (from 6 April 2016) for the time reasonably spent on the case (no VAT is chargeable).

Litigants in person are not immune from costs orders being made against them. As per the comments in ***Barton v Wright Hassall LLP*** **[2018] 1 WLR, 1119, UKSC**, a litigant in person does not form a privileged class for whom the rules are modified or disapplied, and the litigant in person is expected to familiarise himself with the relevant procedure and take legal advice if necessary. Therefore, it is not an excuse for a litigant in person to say "I didn't know" and expect no consequences.

FPR 2010 part 28.3(5) the general rule in financial remedy proceedings is that the court will not make an order requiring one party to pay the costs of another party.

BUT

FPR 2010 part 28.3(6) the court may make an order requiring one party to pay the costs of another party at any stage of the proceedings where it considers it appropriate to do so because of the conduct of a party in relation to the proceedings (whether before or during them)

When does the general rule not apply?

Applications for/under/in relation to:

- MPS/Interim maintenance

- LSPO

- Any other interim order (for example on a preliminary issues, Part 25 applications, disclosure applications etc)

- Applications to strike out, Set aside a financial remedy order or arbitral award on the grounds of mistake and/or non-disclosure

- Notice to Show Cause, Financial remedy appeal

- Costs of third party joined to the proceedings

- Costs of civil proceedings heard together with financial remedy proceedings

- Schedule 1 proceedings

- The "Clean Sheet" Category

- If the general rule does not apply, then the starting point for costs is that costs follow the event, but that presumption may be displaced more easily in a family case than in a civil case:

  - Baker v. Rowe [2009] EWCA Civ 1162 • Gojkovic v Gojkovic (No. 2) [1991] 2 FLR 233

These are the criteria which the court needs to consider when asked to make a costs order in proceedings to which the general rule applies:

(a) any failure by a party to comply with these rules, any order of the court or any practice direction which the court considers relevant; • (b) any open offer to settle made by a party;

(b) whether it was reasonable for a party to raise, pursue or contest a particular allegation or issue;

(c) the manner in which a party has pursued or responded to the application or a particular allegation or issue;

(d) any other aspect of a party's conduct in relation to proceedings which the court considers relevant; and

(e) the financial effect on the parties of any costs order

CHAPTER THIRTY-THREE

DRAFTING APPLICATIONS AND STATEMENTS

Introduction

A paper application in family court proceedings sets the scene for any family court case. The purpose of the application is not only to tell the court what order you are seeking but to tell others too. There will always be at least one respondent (the applicant's opponent) who needs to know what order the applicant is seeking and the reason why it is filed with the court. It is a principal of natural justice that any respondent has an opportunity to oppose the application and put forward their own case. Court procedure allows any respondent to put their case (usually in writing) and give evidence at a court hearing if necessary.

Applications

1. If your client is seeking an order from the family court you will need to complete an application form and file this with the court together with any other relevant papers.

2. The form itself will depend what order is being sought. If the applicant is seeking a care order or supervision order the form is likely to be **Form C110A**. In the case of a private law application **Form C100.** For a non-molestation order it will be **Form FL401** and for a financial order following divorce it be **Form A**. The form will trigger the beginning of court proceedings. Using the correct form is vital. Otherwise, the application will be delayed or even rejected by the court. So take great care should be taken in choosing the form.

3. The content and the drafting of this form is also very important. It is an opportunity to set out the applicant's case at an early stage.

4. The form will be filed and seen by the court, by the opposing party and in the case of private children proceedings, a copy is also sent to CAFCASS.

5. It is not usually possible to file a detailed statement at this point, but the form can be used to good effect. If the applicant chooses to use additional pages this is acceptable. The contents of the application form will be read very early in the process and setting out your case at the beginning can be useful. Amending the form at a later stage can be complicated so it is important that the details are accurate and clear.

6. Once the application form is filed with the Family Court the papers will be considered by a court official known as a 'Gatekeeper'

7. **The Gatekeeper**

The Gatekeeper (a District Judge or Legal Advisor) will decide on whether the application filed by the applicant is suitable to be heard by the Lay magistrates. In practice, many of the uncomplicated children cases are heard by Lay magistrates, as are non molestation and occupation orders. Otherwise, the application will be listed before a District Judge or a Circuit Judge. An application can be transferred to another court at any stage in the proceedings if deemed necessary.

8. **Statements**

In family court proceedings, a witness statement will stand as the party's main evidence to the Judge. The other parent will read the statement before the hearing. Cross examination will be based on what is written in the statement so it is important the contents are accurate. Statements are common in some proceedings and less common in others. For example, statements are usual in care proceedings, injunction cases and some private children applications. They are less common in financial applications.

9. **Who makes and files a statement?**

- A party to proceedings
- Witnesses including experts

10. **General Guidance**

The Rules as to the making and filing of statements are set out in **Part 22 FPR 2010** and **Practice Direction 22A**: as to content and style.

https://www.justice.gov.uk/courts/procedure-rules/family/parts/part_22

The President of the Family Division, Sir Andrew McFarlane, has issued a memorandum setting out how witness statements should be prepared for use in the Family Courts to ensure they meet proper professional standards. The full details can be found below.

https://www.judiciary.uk/wp-content/uploads/2021/11/PFD-memo-on-witness-statements-12112021.pdf

- A witness statement should be factual and state what was seen, heard, or felt by the person writing the statement
- A party can only file a statement if the court directs this
- A statement is the main way of setting out a party's case
- Once evidence has been filed no further evidence/statement is permitted without permission of the court

- Statements can be contemporaneous (parties file at the same time) or consecutive (where one party files first and the other files by way of reply)

- A party may, with the court's permission, file witness statements to support their case

- The court can limit the length and content of the statement

- A party can attach exhibits to their statement to great effect: copies of documents including emails, copies of text messages, photographs, video recordings and audio recordings.

- Recent guidance given by the President of Family Division: **Presidents Memorandum: Witness Statements 10th November 2021**

- A party is required to file their statement with the court and serve a copy on the opposing party, and others if appropriate, eg CAFCASS, Local Authority or experts

- A party usually files a narrative statement. A position statement can be filed at a later stage often prepared to inform the court of a party's case shortly before a court hearing

- A client should be given a copy of the statement to refresh memory in advance of a court hearing

- Affidavits are sworn statements. They are used infrequently and often when the court feels the need to impress on a party or witness the importance of making a statement that is accurate.

11. How to prepare a statement

- The witness statement must be expressed in the first person using the witness's own words

- If a party's address is confidential it can state that only the court knows the address

- Allow the client to have time to consider before signing the statement. It sets out their evidence to the court so the client needs to be fully in agreement with the contents

- Initially map out the points the statement needs to cover and then expand on the important subjects

- The use of headings can be helpful and makes the reading of the statement easier to follow

- It should be brief, without repetition and relevant

- How much is too much? This is a matter of professional judgment but you should lean on the side of brevity. Resist pressure from the client to unduly attack or criticise the other party especially in children cases

- At the end of the document set out a 'statement of truth' as to the contents

- Ensure the statement is filed with the court on time, otherwise the court's permission will be required to file it late

- **Templates** are readily available to the parties. They can be used instead of starting a statement with a blank piece of paper. They are often used by a litigant in person and encouraged in their use by the President of the Family Division. They are available from the court office and downloadable on the internet.

https://www.gov.uk/government/publications/form-c120-witness-statement-template-child-arrangements-parental-dispute

https://www.judiciary.uk/wp-content/uploads/2021/11/PFD-memo-on-witness-statements-12112021.pdf

CHAPTER THIRTY-FOUR

INSTRUCTING COUNSEL

Introduction

In England and Wales, separate sections of the legal profession exist. Barristers can also be referred to as 'counsel'. They are 'members of the Bar. Barristers are not limited to accepting instructions from law firms. Where a barrister is briefed directly by the client it is referred to as 'Direct Access'.

Reasons for Instructing Counsel

- Counsel can provide expertise which the law firm does not possess. This expertise may relate to a specialised area of family law. The Bar consists of specialist advocates and few solicitors have the opportunity to develop the level of advocacy skills and experience possessed by many barristers. Solicitors often find it advantageous to be able to obtain a second opinion from an independent legal practitioner.

- Barristers can provide a very cost-effective service. Barristers, and especially more junior barristers, can provide their services at a much cheaper daily or hourly rate than solicitors of equivalent standing.

Selecting Counsel appropriate for the task

- Many firms have a set of chambers whom they usually brief. If your firm has a good working relationship with a particular barrister, then it is a very good reason to use this barrister if the matter in question falls within the range of the barrister's experience or expertise.

- When choosing barristers, three factors should be taken into account: seniority, specialisation and experience. Seniority normally carries with it a higher price tag. There are two levels of barristers: junior barristers (who vary in experience from being newly qualified to very experienced practitioners) and KCs (who hold the title for their exceptional ability and competence). Fee structures within the Bar vary ranging from junior barristers who may charge as little as a few hundred pounds per day, up to the top KCs at thousands of pounds per day. It is important to brief a barrister in matters involving an issue of law within the barrister's area of specialisation. In order to choose counsel best qualified for the task in hand, you may need to seek advice from others in your firm, or from lawyers in other firms.

Arrange conferences where necessary or appropriate

A pre-trial conference is where the barrister meets the client, discusses their evidence and offers them advice as to the manner in which they may give their evidence. Such conferences can be very helpful in cases where a client is planning to give oral testimony. It may be that no court proceedings have commenced but the client has asked for advice in anticipation of such proceedings. This can take place remotely by Zoom or Teams usually set up by the instructing Solicitor making the arrangements and for counsel and the client to be invited to attend. This will enable action to be taken on matters advised by counsel.

Counsels' fees

- The situation regarding fees for counsel must be clearly understood by all concerned. Disputes relating to fees are one of the two main sources of disagreement between solicitors and members of the Bar. Such disputes can be minimised by ensuring that the situation is clearly explained and understood.

- If the fee is a fixed one - such as a Legal Aid scale fee - or has been negotiated in advance, this should be clearly confirmed with the brief. You will provide the legal aid certificate number with the papers. The responsibility of paying counsel's fees rests with the instructing solicitor. If you have any doubts about the client's ability to pay, or the client's willingness to pay, you should ensure that you have funds on account before counsel is briefed.

- It is also the responsibility of solicitors to remit funds to counsel as soon as counsel has performed the work.

- From time to time, problems arise in relation to paying counsel's fees, either because the client is not forthcoming with funds, or because funds held from the client prove to be insufficient. In such a case, it remains the professional responsibility of the Solicitor to pay counsel's fees, even if the firm has to pay those fees from its own resources.

Style of Brief or Instructions to Counsel

- Instructions can be to advise in writing, to advise in conference or to attend a court hearing (brief). There is no strict form which this document must take, and its contents will depend on the nature of the particular case. Some practical points :

    - Instructions are usually given in chronological order.

    - It is helpful if the brief is in a ring binder which allows pages to be inserted and removed easily.

    - Separate the divisions in the brief with cardboard 'dividers'

    - Original documents such as title deeds, mortgages, signed contracts should not be included in a brief to counsel. There is always a risk that such documents may go astray.

- If there is something that counsel should know about as soon as he or she receives the brief, it should be marked on the outside of the brief, preferably in large red lettering. This is particularly important if there is a time-limit, such as a limitations period due to expire in the near future.

- Identify, on the outside of the brief, hearing dates or dates of other forthcoming court appearances. This enables the barrister, or the barrister's clerk, to ensure that the correct dates are in the barrister's diary and conflicting engagements are avoided.

- It is helpful to identify the individual within the law firm whom the barrister should contact if it is necessary to discuss the matter. This should include the individual's direct telephone number and email address.

- If more than one barrister is briefed in the same case, the brief should also identify, preferably on the outer cover the name of the leader or junior

- Counsel's brief will be updated for each subsequent hearing.

- It is increasingly common for solicitors to brief barristers by email, without providing documents in hard copy.

Content of Brief

- Ensure that the Brief includes everything that Counsel will need. If you are not sure whether or not a particular document is relevant you should include it.

- Include a brief summary of the facts and issues by way of a broad 'over-view' of the case. You should not go into to extensive detail which is set out fully in witness statements and documentary evidence,

- Observations highlighting specific issues potentially problematic should be included which cross-references to witness statements and items of documentary evidence regarded as critically important.

- Instructions are not intended to take the place of proper witness statements. If the Instructing Solicitors are aware of relevant facts which may not emerge from witness statements, it may be convenient to mention these. Except in the very simplest cases, it is unacceptable however merely to summarise the client's instructions without furnishing a proper statement.

- Instructions to advise should also elaborate on precisely what counsel is instructed to do. In the case of a request to provide an opinion, it is often useful for the solicitors to specify precisely the questions and issues which counsel is required to address – advice on evidence, or advice on prospects of success, or advice on some specific legal issue.

Layout of Brief

- Written in third person

- Heading-court proceedings or name of client

- Who you are and for whom you act

- Nature of dispute

- Brief background with relevant events and chronology

- Deadlines-hearing dates-time limits

- Your requirements of the barrister
- Contact details
- Legal Aid reference number

Attendance at court

Traditionally lawyers have accompanied their client in attending court with counsel. The Solicitor would assist counsel in dealing with the client, take notes at the hearing and advise the client after the hearing. The rules have been relaxed over the years to the extent that it is no longer necessary for a solicitor to be present at court with the client. This is a common feature in legal aid cases. If a matter is listed for hearing, a private paying client should be given the option of attending court with counsel but without their solicitor being present. This will save costs for the client. If counsel attends court without a solicitor they are expected to provide a detailed report to their instructing lawyers as to the outcome of the hearing as soon as possible after the hearing.

Direct Access

- The Public Access Rules came into force in July 2004 which permitted members of the public or professional organisations to instruct a barrister directly, without first engaging a Solicitor. In order to represent members of the public on a Direct Access basis, barristers must have undertaken training to the satisfaction of the Bar Standards Board. There will be occasions where it would not be appropriate for a barrister to assist a client directly, in which case he/she will be signposted to a firm of solicitors able to assist.
- The cost of a public access case will depend on the nature of the case. Generally, barristers would work for a fixed fee or alternatively provide an hourly rate if preferred. Services provided

by public access barristers include: advisory work, drafting of documents, correspondence, negotiation, court representation.

https://www.barstandardsboard.org.uk/for-the-public/finding-and-using-a-barrister/how-to-instruct-a-barrister/public-access-guidance-for-lay-clients.html

Barristers' Clerk

Barristers' clerks work as administrators within barrister chambers. They keep chamber diaries up to date, calculate and negotiate fees for the work carried out and ensure every member is informed of their commitments. Other key responsibilities include allocating cases to barristers, considering their expertise, specialisms and availability, managing financial accounts, marketing the chambers and organising meetings between clients, barristers and instructing Solicitor. Clerks have detailed knowledge about the barristers on their list. In recent years and in line with modernisation of the barristers' profession, some barristers no longer employ clerks but manage their fees and time themselves or use modern management structures.

For more information contact Institute of Barristers' Clerks

https://ibc.org.uk

When the brief is returned at short notice

A barrister who wishes to return a brief is permitted to do so in enough time to give another barrister a proper opportunity to take over the case. To enable this to happen, a barrister (or more likely his/her clerk) must inform you as soon as they realise there is a possibility that they will be unable to do the work required. This might happen when a barrister has overrun in an earlier case. There are three options in these circumstances: find another barrister, seek an adjournment or take over conduct of the matter. A decision should be made in consultation with your client.

Complaints against barristers

- Circumstances may still arise that require you to consider making a formal complaint against a barrister in relation to his or her professional conduct. As a general rule, you should only invoke those formal complaint procedures after exhausting all informal options to resolve a dispute or difficulty.

- The Bar Standards Board regulates barristers in England and Wales who are responsible for making sure that the high standards of the profession are maintained. There are two ways to make a complaint about a barrister: If the barrister is acting for you and you are not satisfied with their service, you should contact the Legal Ombudsman. http://www.legalombudsman.org.uk

- If the barrister is not acting for you and you want to complain about their professional conduct, you should contact The Bar Standards Board. http://www.barstandardsboard.org.uk

CHAPTER THIRTY-FIVE

REPORTING IN THE FAMILY COURTS

To make sure that children, vulnerable adults and families are protected from unwanted publicity, restrictions have been put in place to limit what the media can report. A new era for transparency in family court reporting has begun with a pilot scheme that was launched on the 30th January 2023 under the title of Reporting Pilot.

Reporters are generally allowed to attend family court hearings. They do not need to apply or give notice. The rules give a general right of attendance to journalists and legal bloggers, to most, but not all, private hearings.

The Family Procedure Rules 2010 govern the procedure in the Family Court and the High Court.

Under rule 27.10, hearings relating to family matters are generally held in private, meaning members of the public cannot be present.

While accredited media representatives may attend hearings under rule 27.11(2), subject to exceptions, there are strict limits on what they can report.

Under section 12 of the Administration of Justice Act 1960 it may, for example, be a contempt of court to publish information about proceedings relating to children if a court sits in private. Additionally, under section 97(2) of the Children Act 1989, it is an offence to publish information which could identify a child involved in certain proceedings.

Before considering the Reporting Project and the changes it brings about, it may be helpful to look at the position that currently operates in family courts throughout England and Wales. I will do this by asking a series of questions:

Can the media attend every type of case?

No, the media are not allowed to attend:

- any placement or adoption proceedings,
- any conciliation or financial dispute resolution appointments where a judge is helping the parties to reach an agreement within court proceedings typically FDR or FHDRA hearings.

Can the media be excluded from any other cases?

The court can exclude or restrict the media if:

- it is necessary in the interests of any child concerned in, or connected with, the case
- a party or a witness (or a person associated with a party or a witness) needs to be protected – for example, where a witness's safety may be at risk if the media attended court
- the case may be disrupted if the media is present – for example, if there is not enough space in the court room; or
- justice may otherwise be impeded or prejudiced – for example, where there is a risk that a witness will not give full or frank evidence because the media is present.

FPR 27.11(3) defines the limited circumstances in which the court may (of its own motion or on application) exclude a reporter from all or part of a hearing.

How do I know if the media plan to attend my case?

The media does not need to give advance permission from the court.

If the media is attending any part of the proceedings in your case, the court will ask you and the parties involved if you have any concerns. If you do, you could give one of the reasons listed above. Concerns about potential reporting are not a basis for excluding a reporter from attending. The court will then make a decision about whether or not to exclude the media. The court should consider FPR 27.11(3) in deciding whether to exclude the reporter. FPR 27.11(3) requires something more than the fact that the nature of the proceedings is private or that one or more parties would prefer them not to attend. The need to restrict publication of information does not necessarily mean a reporter should be excluded from observing.

Which media representatives are allowed in court?

Only media representatives who are accredited members of the UK Press Card scheme can attend a family court case. They should wear a UK Press Card (displaying their photograph) at all times, so that they can be easily identified by court staff and the parties involved in the case. If a media representative doesn't bring his or her press card to court, he or she will only be permitted to attend proceedings if the court gives specific permission. Recording, filming and photography are not allowed in family courts. The right of attendance applies to accredited media representatives (journalists with a press card) and duly authorised lawyers (qualified lawyers attending for journalistic, research or public legal educational purposes (often known as legal bloggers). The collective term 'reporters' covers both. A legal blogger should provide Form FP301. This is not required for a journalist.

Do we have to answer questions from the media?

No, you do not have to tell the media anything if you do not wish to. If you do speak to them, whether inside or outside the courthouse, you need to know that they might report what you say. You must also remember that in many cases, especially those involving children, there are legal restrictions on what you are allowed to tell people including journalists. There are also restrictions on what documents and evidence used in the proceedings you can show them.

Can we talk about our case outside court?

It is important to be very careful about what you tell people about the case. If you give details that should not be disclosed, you may be guilty of a criminal offence or contempt of court.

What can the media report?

This depends on the type of case:

- In matrimonial cases the media can usually report names and addresses of parties, an outline of the grounds and defences in the case, legal points, and the judge's rulings.

- In matrimonial finance cases the media can usually publish: names, addresses and occupations of parties and witnesses; a concise statement of the grounds of the application and defences raised, submissions on any point of law and the judgment. The media cannot report what has occurred in the proceedings nor information and evidence disclosed in relation to the case by the parties orally or contained in documents filed in the case, unless the court has given permission.

- In children cases, reporting is much more limited. In general, the court needs to give permission for anyone to publish: any details which could identify the child as being the subject of the proceedings, any information about what has taken place, or been said, in court, any information contained in documents in the proceedings.

- In Private Children Act 1989 proceedings, s12 Administration of Justice Act 1960 significantly curtails what can be published. A reporter may attend but report very little without the permission of the court. In those cases a reporter may wish to make an application to report which is usually best dealt with at the end of the hearing. S97 Children Act 1989 precludes the identification of a child as the subject of proceedings during the life of the case.

- In domestic violence cases, the rules on what can be reported vary, depending on the facts of the case. If there are children involved in the case, reporting is likely to be much more restricted than if there are no children involved.

What is the media not allowed to report?

If the media attend a court case, it does not mean that they can report all that is said in court or identify the parties involved. In certain types of cases, there are legal restrictions that the media has to follow.

For example, it is a criminal offence to publish:

- information about a child such as their name, their school or their home address that might enable the identification of a child as being involved in the proceedings; and

- details of any parties or witnesses that could also enable the identification of a child as being involved in the proceedings. There are other reporting restrictions which make it a contempt of court for anyone, including the media, to publish details of what has happened in a court case involving a child's welfare or maintenance. This includes details of what was said by lawyers, the judge, the parties and witnesses, as well as the content of any documents. In some cases, the judge is able to place additional restrictions on reporting. They can also decide to relax some, or all, of the restrictions.

Can the media see any documents that are used in our case?

No, In most cases, the media cannot see any documents unless the judge gives permission. However, in matrimonial or civil partnership matters, it is possible for anyone, including the media, to obtain a copy of the decree nisi/absolute or conditional/final order. In children cases, the parties or their legal representatives are allowed to disclose information to a journalist, as long as they are doing this to get advice and support or to pursue the investigation of a complaint. The journalist still has to follow the reporting restrictions and therefore cannot pass on the information or publish the information to the general public, or a section of the general public.

Review of transparency in the Family Courts

In 2019, the President of the Family Division, Sir Andrew McFarlane, appointed a review panel to investigate transparency in the Family Courts. Amongst other things the panel asked the following questions:

- Is the line currently drawn correctly between, on the one hand, the need for confidentiality for the parties and children whose personal information may be the subject of proceedings in the Family Court, and, on the other hand, the need for the public to have confidence in the work that these courts undertake on behalf of the State and society?

- If not, what steps should be taken to achieve either greater openness or increased confidentiality?

- Any observations on the Practice Guidance: Family Court Anonymisation Guidance issued by the President on 7 December 2018 and the President's Guidance as to reporting in the Family Courts, issued on 29 October 2019.

Sir Andrew published the panel's findings and his recommendations in the October 2021 report, Confidence and Confidentiality: Transparency in the Family Courts.

Sir Andrew said the time had come: "for accredited media representatives and legal bloggers to be able, not only to attend and observe Family Court hearings, but also to report publicly on what they see and hear."

He said: "Openness and confidentiality are not irreconcilable and each is achievable. The aim is to enhance public confidence significantly, whilst at the same time firmly protecting continued confidentiality."

Sir Andrew noted that witnesses to the review panel had referred to the "chilling effect" of section 12 of the 1960 Act (contempt of court). Sir Andrew said: "... the fear of breaching it and the costs involved in litigation have acted as a major disincentive to journalists and others reporting on Family cases." He said it was not for judiciary to consider whether section 12 should be repealed or replaced but that he supported "calls for urgent consideration to be given by government and Parliament to a review of this provision."

The Reporting Pilot

In the October 2021 report, Sir Andrew proposed bringing forward rules to mitigate the impact of section 12, so allowing journalists and legal bloggers to attend and report on Family Court proceedings.

In November 2021, a Transparency Implementation Group was established to carry out these recommendations. The result of this work is the 'Reporting Pilot' .

On 30th January 2023, the Reporting Pilot was launched in the designated courts of Cardiff, Leeds and Carlisle.

The Reporting Pilot would apply to any level of judge of the family court, or in the Family Division of the High Court Initially the Reporting Pilot will begin with district, circuit, and high court judges, and then would be phased to include magistrates at an appropriate point. Depending on the court centre and the level of interest, the types of cases within the pilot may be phased in.

The pilot would run over a period of 12 months and be subject to independent evaluation. The aim of the pilot was to introduce a presumption that legal bloggers and accredited media may report on what they see and hear during family court cases, subject to strict rules of anonymity (the transparency principle). Only so-called 'pilot reporters' would be able to attend and report on proceedings heard in pilot courts.

All reporting would be subject to the principles of protection of the anonymity of any children involved unless the Judge orders otherwise (the anonymity principle).

The ability to report was being piloted to make sure it can be done safely and with minimum disruption to those involved in the cases, and the courts. Judges in these Courts would make a Transparency Order, which set out the rules of what could and could not be reported. The Court may depart from the transparency principle in any case. In deciding whether to restrict reporting, the Court must ensure the rights of the family and parties to a fair trial under Article 6 ECHR and must balance the rights to a private and family life under Article 8 ECHR, and the rights of the press, public and parties under Article 10 ECHR (or any other relevant rights which may be engaged).

Transparency Orders

The Court would consider whether to make a Transparency Order in any case where a pilot reporter attends a hearing (remotely or in person). The Court retains a discretion to direct that there should be no reporting of the case.

There would be a standard form of Transparency Order, but the Court may modify the terms of the standard order as appropriate on the facts of the case. The Court may do so of its own motion, or by invitation.

The Court retained a discretion to (later) vary or discharge the Transparency Order or to direct that there should be no (further) reporting of the case. This discretion may be exercised of the Court's own motion or on application by a party or a pilot reporter.

The rules on what may or may not be reported in a particular case would be set out in a transparency order issued by the court. Each order would take the form of an injunction and reporters would be bound by its terms.

All reporting would be subject to the principle of anonymity in relation to children, family members and other specified parties, unless the court orders otherwise.

The standard Transparency Order would state that it remained in place until any child to whom the proceedings relate reaches the age of 18.

The standard Transparency Order would provide that, in any reporting about the proceedings, the following must not be reported to the public at large, or a section of the public, without the express permission of the Court:

a. The name or date of birth of any subject child in the case;

b. The name of any parent or family member who is a party or who is mentioned in the case, or whose name may lead to the child(ren) being identified;

c. The name of any person who is a party to, or intervening in, the proceedings;

d. The address of any child or family member;

e. The name or address of any foster carer;

f. The school/hospital/placement name or address, or any identifying features of a school of the child;

g. Photographs or images of the child, their parents, carer or any other identifying person, or any of the locations specified above in conjunction with other information relating to the proceedings;

h. The names of any medical professional who is or has been treating any of the children or family member;

i. In cases involving alleged sexual abuse, the details of such alleged abuse;

j. Any other information likely to identify the child as a subject child or former subject child.

Under the standard Transparency Order journalists would be able to identify:

- The local authority/authorities involved in the proceedings
- The director and assistant director of children's services within the local authority (but usually not the social workers working directly with the family, including the team manager, unless the court so orders)
- Senior personnel at Children and Family Court Advisory and Support Service (Cafcass) (but usually not the guardian appointed for the child)
- Any NHS Trust
- Court-appointed experts (but not treating clinicians or medical professionals)
- Legal representatives and judges

- Anyone else named in a published judgment.

Family members

Family members would for the first time be free to speak to journalists reporting under the pilot without being at risk of contempt of court. It would also be permissible for journalists to quote family members in their reporting, as long as the family is effectively anonymised. It would not permit the parties to themselves publish information from the proceedings where this would be restricted by section 12 AJA1960 and/or the rules of court. This included re-publishing any media articles or blogs written about the case under the pilot, where accompanied by comment that may identify the child concerned.

Documents

A reporter who attends a hearing, or who intends to attend a forthcoming hearing, is entitled to see certain documents from a case (but not all documents). They are also entitled to quote from or publish the contents of those documents, subject to effective anonymisation, once a transparency order has been made.

The permitted documents are:

- Documents drafted by advocates (or litigants if a party is self-representing): ie case outlines, skeleton arguments, summaries, position statements, threshold documents and chronologies.

- Any indices from the court bundle.

- Any suitably anonymised orders within the case.

Qualifying cases

The following cases will be part of the Reporting Pilot:

a. All applications for public and private law Orders under Parts II and IV Children Act 1989, including applications to discharge, vary or enforce existing Orders. The pilot will commence with public law cases and shortly thereafter extend to private law cases.

b. All applications for placement orders where the application is made within care proceedings, up to the point at which any placement order is made or the application for a placement order or otherwise is concluded.

c. All applications under the inherent jurisdiction of the High Court, including applications to authorise the deprivation of a child's liberty

The pilot will start with public law cases (such as care order proceedings) and then proceed to include private law cases (for example, child arrangements orders).

Financial remedy proceedings are excluded

The pilot excludes financial remedy cases, such as money claims made on divorce, along with applications under the Family Law Act 1996 eg non molestation orders

The current practice is for courts to restrict the publication of confidential financial information where parties have been compelled to disclose their affairs as part of the proceedings. The transparency of such proceedings continues to be a matter of debate. The Transparency Implementation Group is examining the issue as part of ongoing work to open up the Family Court.

How will the new approach work in practice?

Generally

- The court should let the parties and their legal representatives know that a reporter is intending to attend.
- The court will make arrangements for the reporter to be provided with a link in remote hearings.
- There will be a check reporter's credentials – for journalists this is a UK press card; for legal bloggers practising certificate or letter from their academic institution or Registered Educational Charity such as The Transparency Project, and form FP301.
- There should be confirmation the hearing is one which reporters are permitted to attend (FPR 27.11)
- There should be consideration of whether a reporter should be provided with key documents to aid understanding.
- The media do not need to obtain advance permission from the court.

At the start of the hearing –

- The court should deal with any objections to attendance in the presence of the reporter
- Explore any potential issues regarding reporting – ensure all parties and reporters are agreed on what can be reported. In a Reporting Pilot case the court should ensure that all have the pilot guidance and deal with the terms of the Transparency Order

At the end of the hearing –

- The court will check whether the reporter wishes to make an oral application for permission to report or if a party wishes to make representations.

- The court and the parties should ensure that any order regarding reporting is drawn clearly and provided to the reporter.

- If the court is directing that documents should be shared with a reporter this should be set out in writing with a date for compliance by the party.

BR & Ors, Re (Transparency Order: Finding of Fact Hearing) [2023] EWFC 9

Poole J was dealing with care proceedings relating to 3 families (previously unconnected), all based in the Yorkshire area. He had previously determined that the fact-finding aspects of each set of care proceedings should be heard at a combined hearing, as each case related to allegations of fabricated or induced illness, and involved the children in question being treated at the same hospital (Sheffield Children's Hospital).

Issues

Two of the sets of proceedings had been issued in the Family Court at Leeds, and the third (which bears a non-Leeds case number) had been transferred to Leeds. The relevance of the location is that Leeds is a Transparency Reporting Pilot Court from 30th January 2023. The combined fact-finding was scheduled to last for 11 weeks beginning on 17th January 2023, so that for about 9 of the 11 weeks accredited media representatives and legal bloggers would be able not only to attend the hearing (as is currently permitted in any court), but also to report publicly on what they see and hear (provided the anonymity of the children and families is maintained). Poole J thought it appropriate to adopt the pilot from 17th January 2023 to enable the entire hearing to be reported.

Poole J referred to the President's Guidance on the Reporting Pilot, and the need to balance the parties' rights under the European Convention on Human Rights: in particular, the right to a fair trial (Article 6), the right to private and family life (Article 8) and the right to freedom of expression (Article 10). He reminded himself of s12 of the Human Rights Act 1998, which sets out that the court "must have particular regard to the importance of the Convention right to freedom of expression".

Section 12 of the Administration of Justice Act 1960 prohibits the publication of information relating to proceedings in private relating to children, unless the court orders otherwise. A Transparency Order ("TO") effectively loosens (but does not entirely lift) the restrictions otherwise in place under s12 AJA.

Section 97 of the Children Act 1989 prohibits the publication of material which will is intended to or is likely to identify any child as being involved in proceedings under the Children Act 1989 or Adoption and Children Act 1989, or an address/school as being that of a child involved in any such proceedings. This applies whilst proceedings are on-going, but a TO is typically made until a child is 18.

The leading case law comes from Re S [2004] UKHL 47 and Griffiths v Tickle [2021] EWCA Civ 1882, i.e. the court must balance the rights that favour publication and the rights of the child to respect for its private and family life. Decisions tend to be fact-sensitive.

Decision

Poole J concluded that:

- There is a significant public interest in allowing reporting of family proceedings (para 20(iii));

- Save in exceptional circumstances where it would be particularly difficult to achieve anonymity for the child, the terms of the template TO will strike the right balance between the competing rights (para 20(iv))T the TO is supplemented by the provisions of CA 1989 s97, as it is a criminal offence to publish information likely to identify a child, which offers significant protections against identification (para 20(v))

- Any prohibitions on publication going beyond the standard TO should be limited to avoid undue interference with article 10 rights to freedom of expression (para 20(iv))

- A court can make specific TO directions to reduce the likelihood of 'jigsaw information' (i.e. a situation where someone can combine several pieces of information to identify a child, even if each piece of information individually is insufficient to enable identification to occur) (para 20(vii)). He considered this further in paragraphs 34–35, and declined to make anything other than 'very limited additions to the information that may not be reported already listed in the template TO', noting that pilot reporters are bound to take their responsibilities under s97 very seriously, 'and will naturally be cautious to avoid committing an offence'. To assist reporters in avoiding jigsaw identification he added a schedule of 7 pieces of information which could give rise to the jigsaw identification process (para 38)

- Sometimes it may be appropriate to relate the template TO if there is information which would generally not be published, but in the particular circumstances of a case there is an especially strong public interest in it being reported (para 20(viii)).

- A court can make a TO when there are or may be pending criminal proceedings, but generally reporting should be prevented until the investigation/criminal proceedings have concluded, to avoid prejudicing them (para 20(ix)).

He therefore made a TO in the template format, but with two variations:

(1) No reporting would be permitted until criminal proceedings had concluded and/or the police or the CPS had determined criminal proceedings would not be brought and no further action taken. The only exception was reporting of the facts that the reporting project has been adopted for this hearing, how the court dealt with the arguments made, and the existence of the TO.

(2) He attached a confidential schedule with the names of all relevant family members (including the children) to reduce the risk that someone would be named inadvertently given the large number of parties/children.

Additional points which required resolution were determined as follows:

- Pilot reporters were permitted to attend either in person or remotely (as this was to be a hybrid hearing)
- Given the large volume of documentation, he directed that pilot reporters were entitled to:

  (i) Opening and closing position statements or skeleton arguments;

  (ii) The indices to the hearing bundles

  Any other documentation would have to be requested and a decision taken at that point
- Pilot reporters are entitled to share information with each other and 4 named members of the Transparency Project are entitled to share information with each other (this should enable a 'job share' in relation to reporting)

- One specific hospital was named (Sheffield Children's Hospital), as it is a 'significant common feature' to the three cases

Poole J noted that as pilot reporters became more familiar with the case there be applications to vary the TO (none of the pilot reporters had seen any documentation at the time the TO was being considered). Those would have to be determined at suitable points as and when they arose (para 44)

That's where we were

On Monday 29 January 2024 the Transparency Implementation Group Reporting Pilot (TIG), which for the first time made it the default position that the media could report on family cases, will be extended to 16 courts across the country.

The courts that will be taking part in the pilot from Monday 29 January are:

- North West: Liverpool, Manchester
- North East: West Yorkshire, Kingston-upon-Hull
- Midlands: Nottingham, Stoke, Derby, Birmingham
- London: Central Family Court, East London, West London
- South West: Dorset, Truro
- South East: Luton, Guildford, Milton Keynes

President of the Family Division Sir Andrew McFarlane said:

> "Extending the reporting pilot to family courts across the country is a huge step in the judiciary's ongoing work to increase transparency and improve public confidence and

> understanding of the family justice system. After a pioneering year of reporting from Leeds, Cardiff and Carlisle journalists and legal bloggers will be allowed to report from a further sixteen courts."
>
> "We hope that in extending the pilot further we can continue to understand the impact that family court reporting has. I would like to urge the media to read the guidance and come to the family courts to see the vital and challenging work that is done there, and to report on the cases and issues that are so important."

On Monday 29th January 2024 the Children Reporting Pilot expanded to a list of new courts across England and Wales, and a new Financial Remedy Reporting Pilot began. Overall this will vastly increase the potential for reporters to observe and write about the work of the family court, by reducing the number of barriers to attempting such work in those courts.

So as from February 2024

Courts where Reporting Pilots are in operation:

Children cases: Most public law and private law proceedings before judges and magistrates: Cardiff, Carlisle & Leeds

Most public law proceedings before judges: Liverpool, Manchester, West Yorkshire, Hull, Nottingham, Stoke, Derby, Birmingham, Dorset, Truro, Luton, Guildford, Milton Keynes, Central London, East London and West London.

The pilot has now encompassed private law children cases in all pilot courts including those before magistrates courts

For Financial remedy cases: Central Family Court, Leeds & Birmingham
The pilot is expected to extend to High Court level at the Royal Courts of Justice from November 2024

Since the pilot was launched Mrs Justice Lieven has confirmed that there have been no complaints about the identification of families.

The pilot has only been tested in urban areas and so rural areas, such as Cornwall, are yet to be explored fully. In addition, the clear intention of Rt Hon. Sir Andrew McFarlane was to restrict the reporting to pilot reporters so expansion to other members of the public is not likely at this stage.

For the first time, journalists and bloggers are now able to report on court cases involving financial issues between divorcing married couples and civil partners, as a transparency pilot launches in the Financial Remedies Court.

The rollout began 29th January 2024, the same day as the wider pre-existing family court transparency pilot covering public children cases, hitherto restricted to three courts is broadened out to cover a further sixteen, encompassing half the family courts in England and Wales.

In the latest move to improve transparency and accountability within the family court system, reporting on proceedings in the Financial Remedies Court can take place at the Central Family Court in London, as well as in Leeds and Birmingham.

As part of the pilot, cause lists for all Financial Remedies Courts including cases heard at the Royal Courts of Justice, will name the parties and state that the proceedings involve financial remedies subject, of course to court-issued transparency orders.

However, Financial Dispute Resolution (FDR) hearings are not included as part of the pilot. These hearings will remain completely under wraps to anyone outside the courtroom.

In **Tickle v Father and Ors [2023] EWHC 2446,** Lieven J succinctly draws together and summarises the relevant case law ([22-41]) and principles ([42-52]) in this area. This judgment perhaps also highlights the existence of misunderstanding, even amongst parts of the judiciary, of the existing provisions relating to transparency in the Family Courts, including the prima facie right of the press to attend hearings held in private [6].

Out of the 43 family courts in England and Wales 19 are now participating in the Transparency Pilot.

PILOT SCHEME IN FINANCIAL REMEDY PROCEEDINGS

As with the children cases pilot, a pilot scheme will be established in respect of financial remedy cases. The pilot encompasses:

a. Applications for financial remedies upon divorce;

b. Applications under Schedule 1 of the Children Act 1989;

c. Applications under Part III of the Matrimonial and Family Proceedings Act1984.

Launch date

The pilot was launched on 29 January 2024 and will run for a period 12 months. Cases at High Court level in the Royal Courts of Justice shall, in principle, be included in the pilot from 4 November 2024.

Listing

Cause lists for all FRC courts, including cases heard at the Royal Courts of Justice, will name the parties and state that the proceedings involve financial remedies.

Where the hearing is a FDR, the cause list shall state that no reporter is entitled to attend (FPR 27.11(a)).

Attendance

As at present, reporters will be allowed to attend and report on what they see and hear in court, save that they shall not be permitted to attend a FDR. The details of any reporter attending a hearing should appear on the face of the court order.

The court retains a discretion to permit attendance by a person who is other than a reporter; FPR 27.11(2)(b). The court also retains a discretion to exclude a reporter under FPR 27.11(3), but this should only be done for specific reasons, and upon consideration of PD27B.

Reporters are encouraged to inform the court and the parties in advance of their intention to attend and report on a particular hearing.

Transparency Orders: When and How

Upon an accredited journalist being present, the court is essentially concerned with two questions: (1) whether to make the Transparency Order at all and (2) what terms on which to make the Transparency Order. Of course, it may be that conditions imposed mitigate concerns as to whether a Transparency Order should be made.

1. <u>Whether to make the order at all</u>

When the court is considering the former question, the Court retains a discretion to order that no reporting may take place. In so doing, the Court will balance the parties' Article 6 and 8 ECHR rights (to a fair trial and a private and family life) against the Article 10 ECHR right to freedom of expression. The Court's discretion is maintained and therefore the Order may be varied, or indeed, it may be ordered that no further reporting may take place. Importantly, whilst the child's best interests will be an important consideration, they are not the paramount or only factor. Instead, the child's best interests must be balanced against other rights and the wider considerations surrounding the public interest of reporting cases in the Family Courts.

The considerations the Court will take into account when deciding whether reporting should take place can be found in the guidance and in Mrs Justice Lieven's judgment in **Tickle v Father and Ors [2023] EWHC 2446 (Fam)**. Crucially, although adjournment is possible Mrs Justice Lieven emphasised that adjournment in and of itself is an intrusion upon reporting rights and should not be treated as a normal case management decision (see paragraph [51]).

2. <u>What should be the terms of the Order</u>

A standard form Order has been produced and a Word version is attached to the Reporting Pilot Guidance. This is a 'standard form' Transparency Order, and the Court may modify the terms of the order appropriate to each case.

CHAPTER THIRTY-SIX

THIRTY-THREE COMMON QUESTIONS ASKED BY CLIENTS IN FAMILY CASES

Divorce

Question 1: I understand that the divorce law has changed recently. Are the grounds for divorce the same as before?

Answer: Until 6th April 2022 a party seeking divorce had to satisfy the court that the legal test of irretrievable breakdown was met, by citing one or more of 'five factors': unreasonable behaviour, adultery, or desertion. separation for two years with consent and five years separation. The Divorce, Dissolution and Separation Act 2020 has reformed the law on divorce from 6th April 2022 by removing the requirement to provide evidence of 'conduct' or 'separation' and replacing it with a simple requirement to provide a statement of irretrievable breakdown of the marriage or civil partnership, or to obtain a judicial separation. The new law has also removed the ability to defend the decision to divorce or end the civil partnership. It also allows for the first time, joint applications for divorce, dissolution, and separation, meaning that couples can now apply together.

Question 2: How long does it take to be divorced?

Answer: The new law has introduced a new minimum overall time frame of six months (26 weeks) made up of a 'minimum period' of twenty weeks in divorce proceedings between the start of proceedings and when the applicant may apply for a conditional order. The current minimum time period between the conditional order and final order is six weeks. This ensures that there is a period of reflection and provides an opportunity for couples to agree the practical arrangements for the future.

Question 3: How much does it cost to be divorced?

Answer: With the procedure itself being streamlined and the majority of divorces being processed online, one would expect the cost of the divorce to be reduced in time. The court fee is £593. Solicitors have been charging fees in the region of £750–1000 plus the court fees, but much will depend on the law firm involved.

Question 4: Is the terminology the same since the divorce law has changed?

Answer: There have been a number of changes in terminology:

'Petition' has become 'Application', 'Petitioner' has become 'Applicant', 'Decree Nisi' has become 'Conditional Order' and 'Decree Absolute' has become 'Final Order'. This makes the language simpler and is intended to be more accessible to the general public.

Question 5: What documents are needed to commence divorce proceedings?

Answer: The original marriage certificate or a certified copy, the divorce application (known as Form D8) and the court fee.

Question 6: Does it matter who starts the divorce?

Answer: No. A divorce application can be filed individually or jointly with your spouse.

Question 7: When am I considered divorced?

Answer: On the granting of the Final Order, previously known as the Decree Absolute.

Cohabitation

Question 8: What is a common law marriage?

Answer: There is no such thing.

Question 9: What if my partner leaves and stops paying the bills?

Answer: This depends on whether the bills are in joint names, in your name or your partner's name that has left. In joint names you will be both individually and jointly liable for the outstanding debts. If it is in your partners name he or she will be liable.

Question 10: We are not married and we live in my partner's home. Am I entitled to anything?

Answer: There is no simple answer to this. The law gives no automatic rights to a partner in these circumstances, but if you contributed towards the deposit on a purchase or have provided money for significant improvement to the house, you may have a claim. It is important that the details are considered carefully

Question 11: What if my partner will not leave our shared property?

Answer: If you have not entered into an agreement as to how long you are going to live together and separate, then when coming to separate and leaving a property that will depend on how the property is owned or rented. If it is in joint names, then it may be hard in the short term to enforce someone to leave the property. In the long term, you may need the court's assistance. Careful consideration of the options available is required. It can depend on whether there is a threat of violence itself and if there are children at the property.

Question 12: If we have been living together, but have not married, does everything have to be split 50/50?

Answer: Not necessarily. If you have decided something about the house you live in or property you own and that has been recorded on the deeds, then it has to be followed. However, it can sometimes be challenged. If not, there are different areas of law that govern this subject and it can depend on your circumstances. It is possible that someone ends up with nothing.

Private Children cases

Question 13: What is parental responsibility?

Answer: There is no legal definition of parental responsibility. It includes the rights and responsibility to make welfare decisions for a child such as education, health, religion, where are child lives. However, this is not an extensive list.

Question 14: How do I gain parental responsibility?

Answer: A mother obtains parental responsibility by giving birth. A father, however, has this responsibility only if he is married to the mother or has acquired legal responsibility for the child through one of the following routes:

- Jointly registering the birth of the child with the mother
- A parental responsibility agreement with the mother
- A parental responsibility order made by the court
- A child arrangements order or a special guardianship order

15. Question: What is custody and access?

Answer: These terms are not terms now recognised by the family court in England and Wales. We have referred to residence and contact but even more recently these terms have been overtaken by expressions under a Child Arrangements order

Question 16: What happens to the children if we are split up and we are not married?

Answer: It does not make any difference if you are married or not. The important things are to have parental responsibility and to consider the childrens' welfare needs.

Question 17: Can you stop a violent ex-partner from seeing his child?

Answer: After the implementation of the Children and Families Act 2014 there is a presumption that contact with both parents is in the best interests of the child. Although a parent could stop contact with a violent ex-partner, they cannot stop them applying to the court for a Child Arrangements Order to facilitate contact with their child. If an application was made the court would have to decide if it is suitable to allow contact with the ex-partner. It does not always follow that because they were violent partner they were a violent parent.

Question 18: Can I move abroad with my children?

Answer: You cannot move children out of the country without the other parent's consent. The first step is to try to obtain the other parent's consent to the move. If consent cannot be obtained voluntarily an application has to be made to the court for 'permission to remove from the jurisdiction'

Question 19: Will child maintenance payments stop if I remarry?

Answer: Child maintenance is a payment made by an absent parent for their child. Payments are not made for the ex-partner and as such your relationship status has no bearing on the continuance of the payments. An absent parent has an ongoing legal obligation to maintain their child until they attain the age of 18.

Question 20: How much child maintenance should I pay?

Answer: This area is governed by statute and the easiest way to find out how much you are liable to pay is to look up the Child Maintenance Service website.

Finances and Property matters following divorce

Question 21: How do financial divorce settlements work?

Answer: A financial settlement is the agreement you reach with your former partner regarding the division of your money, property and other assets. The courts set the details of this agreement and make it a binding financial order. When the courts draw up financial settlements, they take certain key factors into consideration. Chief among these are the arrangements for any children of the marriage. In particular, the court will want to know where they will live in future so their housing needs can be properly assessed. Another major factor will be the length of the marriage. The longer it lasted, the greater the settlement the court will order. Generally speaking, marriages which have lasted less than five years are considered short; those that have lasted more than fourteen years would be considered longer marriages. An additional important consideration is the specifics of each party's finances. Each half of the couple will need to fill in a signed statement called a Form E which sets out their future income and financial needs.

Question 22: How much spousal maintenance will I have to pay?

Answer: There is no set formula for calculating spousal maintenance. There are a number of factors which contribute towards the calculation of spousal maintenance including needs and affordability. Maintenance can always be varied upwards and downwards as circumstances change eg the paying party is made redundant. Maintenance comes to an end automatically if the person receiving receiving it remarries. It does not come to an an automatically if the person receiving maintenance stats to cohabit unless the final order in the financial proceedings provides for that eventuality.

Question 23: How long will I have to pay maintenance for in divorce proceedings?

Answer: In relation to children, an absent parent should broadly regard themselves as being liable until the child has concluded full time education. Spousal maintenance duration will depend upon the length of the marriage and whether or not there are dependent. For example, if the marriage is short and there are no children, the likelihood is that no maintenance will be payable or only payable for a short time. The court has a duty to consider whether a clean break is appropriate and if so, when this can be achieved without undue hardship.

Question 24: What is the position regarding pensions following divorce?

Answer: Pensions are an important part of a financial settlement. Pensions are likely to be a significant issue if the marriage is long and /or there are children of the relationship. Pensions will be less important if the marriage is short, there are no children and/or the parties are relatively young.

Question 25: Is it always a 50/50 division of assets following divorce?

Answer: The starting point is usually 50/50 but the court has a checklist of factors to consider whether equality would be a fair outcome. If there are dependant children housing them will be the most influential factor.

Question 26: Are prenuptial agreements legally binding?

Answer: Recent case law asserts that the likelihood is a properly drafted agreement entered into in appropriate circumstances will be upheld in a future divorce. Tailored advice is imperative on the subject in order to obtain the most effective result.

Domestic Abuse

Question 27: Can I get my partner removed from the house if (s)he's violent?

Answer: It depends on the facts but no-one can be expected to live in the same house as a violent partner. The courts will always be open to protect a victim from a violent partner. Urgent applications can be made to the court to stop a violent partner behaving badly and orders can be made to remove the person concerned from the house where you live. This is, of course, in addition to assistance you can receive from the police and the criminal courts by way of bail conditions.

Question 28: What protection is available to me if my partner is seriously abusive towards me?

Answer: A non-molestation order and an occupation order is available. Once again it depends on the fact. Both orders can involve the perpetrator being arrested by the police should there be any breach of the order.

Public Children Law Cases – Care proceedings

Question 29: Can the local Authority remove my child without a court order?

Answer: No, the Local Authority (LA) cannot remove a child from your care unless you consent to this (usually in writing) or if it obtains a court order. Even if you consent to the removal, you can withdraw your consent, forcing the LA to obtain a court order.

Question 30: What does the local Authority have to show in order to obtain a court order to remove my child?

Answer: The court can make a number of court orders to remove a child from your care:

1. **Emergency Protection Order** where the court must be satisfied that the child is at risk of or is suffering harm. An EPO will last for a period of 8 days although the LA can apply for an extension to that time. This order can be made in the absence of the parent.

2. **Interim Care Order** is a temporary order and lasts up to 8 weeks at first, but can be extended. The court must have **reasonable grounds** to believe that the child has suffered or is at risk of suffering significant harm as a result of the care provided by the parents.

3. **Final Care Order** the court the court must be satisfied that the child is suffering or is likely to suffer significant harm and the likelihood of harm is attributable to the care provided by the parent. The future care of the child will be decided on what's best for the child.

Question 32: If my child is removed from my care under a court order, do I have the right to have regular contact?

Answer: Yes, the LA have a duty to promote contact between the parent and the child unless there is good reason for not doing so. The level of contact and arrangements will be agreed with the LA. A parent can apply to the court if she/he is not satisfied with the the LA's proposals of contact.

Question 33: Will an adoption order be made automatically if a final care order is made?

Answer: No, the parents can consent to an adoption order. If they object, the LA will have to prove that the parents are 'withholding their consent unreasonably'

MORE BOOKS BY LAW BRIEF PUBLISHING

'A Practical Guide to Confiscation and Restraint'
by Narita Bahra QC, John Carl Townsend, David Winch

'A Practical Guide to the Law of Forests in Scotland' by Philip Buchan

'A Practical Guide to Health and Medical Cases in Immigration Law'
by Rebecca Chapman & Miranda Butler

'A Practical Guide to Bad Character Evidence for Criminal Practitioners
by Aparna Rao

'A Practical Guide to Extradition Law post-Brexit' by Myles Grandison et al

'A Practical Guide to Hoarding and Mental Health for Housing Lawyers'
by Rachel Coyle

'A Practical Guide to Psychiatric Claims in Personal Injury – 2nd Edition'
by Liam Ryan

'Stephens on Contractual Indemnities' by Richard Stephens

'A Practical Guide to the EU Succession Regulation' by Richard Frimston

'A Practical Guide to Solicitor and Client Costs – 2nd Edition' by Robin Dunne

'Constructive Dismissal – Practice Pointers and Principles' by Benjimin Burgher

'A Practical Guide to Religion and Belief Discrimination Claims in the Workplace'
by Kashif Ali

'A Practical Guide to the Law of Medical Treatment Decisions' by Ben Troke

'Fundamental Dishonesty and QOCS in Personal Injury Proceedings: Law and Practice' by Jake Rowley

'A Practical Guide to the Law in Relation to School Exclusions'
by Charlotte Hadfield & Alice de Coverley

'A Practical Guide to Divorce for the Silver Separators' by Karin Walker

'The Right to be Forgotten – The Law and Practical Issues' by Melissa Stock

'A Practical Guide to Planning Law and Rights of Way in National Parks, the Broads and AONBs' by James Maurici QC, James Neill et al

'A Practical Guide to Election Law' by Tom Tabori

'A Practical Guide to the Law in Relation to Surrogacy' by Andrew Powell

'A Practical Guide to Claims Arising from Fatal Accidents – 2nd Edition'
by James Patience

'A Practical Guide to the Ownership of Employee Inventions – From Entitlement to Compensation' by James Tumbridge & Ashley Roughton

'A Practical Guide to Asbestos Claims' by Jonathan Owen & Gareth McAloon

‘A Practical Guide to Stamp Duty Land Tax in England and Northern Ireland’ by Suzanne O’Hara
‘A Practical Guide to the Law of Farming Partnerships’ by Philip Whitcomb
‘Covid-19, Homeworking and the Law – The Essential Guide to Employment and GDPR Issues’ by Forbes Solicitors
‘Covid-19 and Criminal Law – The Essential Guide’ by Ramya Nagesh
‘Covid-19 and Family Law in England and Wales – The Essential Guide’ by Safda Mahmood
‘A Practical Guide to the Law of Unlawful Eviction and Harassment – 2nd Edition’ by Stephanie Lovegrove
‘Covid-19, Brexit and the Law of Commercial Leases – The Essential Guide’ by Mark Shelton
‘A Practical Guide to Costs in Personal Injury Claims – 2nd Edition’ by Matthew Hoe
‘A Practical Guide to the General Data Protection Regulation (GDPR) – 2nd Edition’ by Keith Markham
‘Ellis on Credit Hire – Sixth Edition’ by Aidan Ellis & Tim Kevan
‘A Practical Guide to Working with Litigants in Person and McKenzie Friends in Family Cases’ by Stuart Barlow
‘Protecting Unregistered Brands: A Practical Guide to the Law of Passing Off’ by Lorna Brazell
‘A Practical Guide to Secondary Liability and Joint Enterprise Post-Jogee’ by Joanne Cecil & James Mehigan
‘A Practical Guide to the Pre-Action RTA Claims Protocol for Personal Injury Lawyers’ by Antonia Ford
‘A Practical Guide to Neighbour Disputes and the Law’ by Alexander Walsh
‘A Practical Guide to Forfeiture of Leases’ by Mark Shelton
‘A Practical Guide to Coercive Control for Legal Practitioners and Victims’ by Rachel Horman
‘A Practical Guide to the Law of Driverless Cars – Second Edition’ by Alex Glassbrook, Emma Northey & Scarlett Milligan
‘A Practical Guide to TOLATA Claims’ by Greg Williams
‘A Practical Guide to Elderly Law – 2nd Edition’ by Justin Patten
‘A Practical Guide to Responding to Housing Disrepair and Unfitness Claims’ by Iain Wightwick

'A Practical Guide to the Law of Bullying and Harassment in the Workplace' by Philip Hyland
'How to Be a Freelance Solicitor: A Practical Guide to the SRA-Regulated Freelance Solicitor Model' by Paul Bennett
'A Practical Guide to Prison Injury Claims' by Malcolm Johnson
'A Practical Guide to the Small Claims Track – 2nd Edition' by Dominic Bright
'A Practical Guide to Advising Clients at the Police Station' by Colin Stephen McKeown-Beaumont
'A Practical Guide to Antisocial Behaviour Injunctions' by Iain Wightwick
'Practical Mediation: A Guide for Mediators, Advocates, Advisers, Lawyers, and Students in Civil, Commercial, Business, Property, Workplace, and Employment Cases' by Jonathan Dingle with John Sephton
'The Mini-Pupillage Workbook' by David Boyle
'A Practical Guide to Crofting Law' by Brian Inkster
'A Practical Guide to the Law of Domain Names and Cybersquatting' by Andrew Clemson
'A Practical Guide to the Law of Gender Pay Gap Reporting' by Harini Iyengar
'NHS Whistleblowing and the Law' by Joseph England
'Employment Law and the Gig Economy' by Nigel Mackay & Annie Powell
'A Practical Guide to Noise Induced Hearing Loss (NIHL) Claims' by Andrew Mckie, Ian Skeate, Gareth McAloon
'An Introduction to Beauty Negligence Claims – A Practical Guide for the Personal Injury Practitioner' by Greg Almond
'Intercompany Agreements for Transfer Pricing Compliance' by Paul Sutton
'Zen and the Art of Mediation' by Martin Plowman
'A Practical Guide to the SRA Principles, Individual and Law Firm Codes of Conduct 2019 – What Every Law Firm Needs to Know' by Paul Bennett
'A Practical Guide to Adoption for Family Lawyers' by Graham Pegg
'A Practical Guide to Industrial Disease Claims' by Andrew Mckie & Ian Skeate
'A Practical Guide to Conducting a Sheriff Court Proof' by Andrew Stevenson
'A Practical Guide to Vicarious Liability' by Mariel Irvine
'A Practical Guide to Applications for Landlord's Consent and Variation of Leases' by Mark Shelton
'A Practical Guide to Relief from Sanctions Post-Mitchell and Denton' by Peter Causton

'A Practical Guide to Equity Release for Advisors' by Paul Sams
'A Practical Guide to Financial Services Claims' by Chris Hegarty
'The Law of Houses in Multiple Occupation: A Practical Guide to HMO Proceedings' by Julian Hunt
'Occupiers, Highways and Defective Premises Claims: A Practical Guide Post-Jackson – 2nd Edition' by Andrew Mckie
'A Practical Guide to Financial Ombudsman Service Claims' by Adam Temple & Robert Scrivenor
'A Practical Guide to Running Housing Disrepair and Cavity Wall Claims: 2nd Edition' by Andrew Mckie & Ian Skeate
'A Practical Guide to Holiday Sickness Claims – 2nd Edition' by Andrew Mckie & Ian Skeate
'Arguments and Tactics for Personal Injury and Clinical Negligence Claims' by Dorian Williams
'A Practical Guide to Drone Law' by Rufus Ballaster, Andrew Firman, Eleanor Clot
'A Practical Guide to Compliance for Personal Injury Firms Working With Claims Management Companies' by Paul Bennett
'RTA Allegations of Fraud in a Post-Jackson Era: The Handbook – 2nd Edition' by Andrew Mckie
'RTA Personal Injury Claims: A Practical Guide Post-Jackson' by Andrew Mckie
'On Experts: CPR35 for Lawyers and Experts' by David Boyle
'An Introduction to Personal Injury Law' by David Boyle

www.ingramcontent.com/pod-product-compliance
Lightning Source LLC
LaVergne TN
LVHW052303200926
848481LV00002B/447
* 9 7 8 1 9 1 6 6 9 8 5 3 6 *